# The Joy of Sax

A Quest for Harmony and Wellbeing In Three Continents

**Bob Swain**

Copyright © 2022 Bob Swain

All Rights Reserved

ISBN: 9798754924079

**Dedicated to the memory of John Coltrane and all the great musicians who have inspired and enriched my life**

# CONTENTS

Blowing At The Altar of Saint John Coltrane     7
– Free the Spirit

Music Is Seriously Good For Your Health     25
– Play Your Way to Wellbeing

Back To School     37
– Musical Beginnings

A Taste For Travel     52
– Setting The Stage

Sax At Sixty     65
– Now or Never

Escape To Sicily     90
– A New Life in the Mediterranean

O Sole Mio     108
– Music and Gelato under the Italian Sun

| | |
|---|---|
| Intermezzo<br>— Duets with Björn | 129 |
| American Odyssey<br>— On The Road Again | 136 |
| Birth of the Cool<br>— A Road Trip Back to the Roots | 160 |
| Intermezzo II<br>— A Brief Return | 173 |
| Into The Jungle<br>— Asian Trails | 176 |
| Cambodia<br>— The Zen of Sax | 188 |
| New Guru New Message<br>— The Brighton Connection | 204 |
| The Music Goes On<br>— Rocking All Over The World | 219 |

BOB SWAIN

# CHAPTER ONE

## Blowing At The Altar of Saint John Coltrane – Free the Spirit

It's the ultimate shrine to the greatest saxophone player who ever lived. And here I am letting loose a torrent of notes in front of the house band only a matter of months after taking the rash decision that this would be my year of sax – the year I turned sixty and the year to fulfil a teenage dream by finally learning to play. And for some crazy reason I decided to turn up the heat by promising myself I'd play a real gig within the first year or two. I must be mad.

We're inside an old shop front in San Francisco's Fillmore district surrounded by brightly painted icons of the one and only John Coltrane. I've been sitting at the back nursing my soprano for the past hour as a string of great horn players step up to the microphone to blast the congregation with solo after solo dedicated to the great man. There's Archbishop Franzo King, the Reverend James Haqq, the Reverend Franzo King Jr and a host of others inspired by the spirit within to take part in this incredible Sunday service.

Then there's all the great musicians on other instruments. The Archbishop's daughter, the Reverend Wanika Stephens, is playing a mean bass while his grandson Carl turns out to be an absolute powerhouse on drums – eerily reminiscent of Coltrane's long-term percussion partner Elvin Jones. Then a large board is laid on the floor and Minister of Tap Megan Haungs steps up to dance. It's not quite as bizarre as you might think as she glides with the beat, adding yet another layer to the complex rhythms beneath the horns.

By now my wife Angela has stepped out to the front of the congregation and started dancing too – a much-appreciated contribution that later received an honourable mention in the sermon.

Despite the simmering atmosphere around me, the best I can do is quietly join in while seated in the back row, desperately hoping none of these incredible musicians will actually hear the dreadful squeaking noise I'm making. The keyboard player is a young guy called Dylan who has been gently encouraging me ever since I walked through the door an hour or so earlier. "Get out your horn, man. Join in."

A short while later, he leans across once again to whisper. "This one's in C sharp minor, man. Why not play along?"

Blimey, I think to myself. I didn't realise I had to know any scales – especially not the hard ones. And does he mean C sharp on piano or saxophone? One of the few things I'd learned so far was that these were not the same thing.

Gulp. What am I going to do? What am I even doing here? I thought I'd be able to make it up as I went along.

So that's just what I do. Picking out a scattering of notes at random that I hope might fit. Some of them do and some of them don't. But it doesn't really matter too much because everyone else is playing at the same time and if I play quietly enough, nobody will actually hear me.

Encouraged by Angela's enthusiastic gyrations I even get to my feet and start swaying to the groove. All goes well until I see a helpful young lady with a microphone heading straight towards me. I stare at her in sheer panic. She smiles and holds the mike right in front of my horn. There's nothing for it but to wing it and play like I mean every note. If I play with enough enthusiasm then maybe they'll just think I'm so good that I don't need to restrict myself to the notes of C sharp minor. I'm sure Coltrane never did!

My consolation at the time was half a quote from Miles Davis who famously said there's no such thing as a wrong note. It's just as well I didn't know the second part where he went on the say that it's only the note you play next that makes the first note right or wrong. All very well so long as I only ever have to play the one note! Needless to say my style was not quite so economical.

And that's pretty much how my first true public saxophone performance came about – 18 months ahead of schedule – leading the free jazz ensemble at Sunday Worship right there in San Francisco.

Although our initial impression of the old store was fairly modest – once you stepped inside the Saint John Will-I-Am African Orthodox Church you were inside an alternate and seductively welcoming universe. Walls were adorned with stunning icons of the late giant of jazz painted by the Reverend Mark Dukes, Coltrane's eyes gazing out from half a dozen highly coloured panels as the congregation gathered for what can only be described as the best Sunday jazz concert in town - with just a little preaching on the side.

But the preaching that day – delivered by Reverend Wanika – was right on the button for any jazz fan. The focus throughout was on the remarkable spirit of Coltrane's music. And who can argue with that? This was certainly the first Christian sermon I ever heard that also dealt with the concept of Boddhisatva – the spiritual journey to Buddhahood. Followers of the Church identify this process with Coltrane's musical journey – a life-long quest for the spirit within through a style famously described by jazz critics at the time as anti-jazz (John Tynan) or more positively as sheets of sound (Ira Gitler).

He was inspired just as much by spiritual trance and non-western cultural influences as he was by Lester Young or Louis Armstrong. As the journey raced off at an increasingly frantic pace (he died in 1967 at just 40 years old) he left any idea of traditional jazz as foot-tapping entertainment way behind – together with many of the more traditional fans. But the sheer energy of his later free jazz work fed increasingly on a spiritual dimension that he had in common with religious practices for millennia past.

Reverend Wanika's sermon recounted the meeting between Coltrane and his record producer just three days before his death when he was asked if he had any suggestions for the title of his final album.

"Expression," he said. "And no other words on the cover except the titles and the names of the musicians."

By then he had said it all. And at the end he knew the most important thing was expression. And that's why his music means so much to so many.

When I first discovered him at the age of 15, he was exactly what I needed. Following hot on the heels of precocious dabbling in books by Jean-Paul Sartre, James Joyce, Herman Hesse and Karl Marx, I was ready for music to take a swerve into the unknown. Along with Coltrane the haul took in the likes of Miles Davis, Igor Stravinsky, Ravi Shankar, field recordings of obscure Delta Blues singers and West African kora ensembles.

Coltrane is the one musician who has remained something close to a divinity for me ever since – so I guess if anyone's going to be a sucker for what this utterly unique church has to offer then it has to be me.

My first introduction was with his remarkable reworking of My Favourite Things from The Sound of Music. If you've not heard his original studio version then drop everything and find a way to listen right now.

It may seem bizarre for a show tune to be the signature piece for a spiritual guru and the god of saxophone players. And indeed it did earn Coltrane his only-ever hit record in the American singles charts. But its deceptively simple structure also takes the listener on a wonderful drifting, meditative journey through time and space. It's a piece Coltrane went on to revisit literally hundreds of times during his career, exploring every nook and cranny of its modulations between major and minor chords in lilting 3/4 time.

Its journey begins with 21-year-old McCoy Tyner on piano, joined after a few seconds by Coltrane's soprano. The instrument was an unusual choice at the time as it had rarely been used in jazz since Sydney Bechet back in the 1920s and 30s. All of Coltrane's previous recordings had been on tenor but he would increasingly turn to the soprano from that point on.

Together with Tyner, he takes the tune for a leisurely spin around the block, stating the theme together with Steve Davis on bass and Elvin Jones on drums. Then Tyner gets to take centre stage with a majestic piano section, never in a rush, played with absolute precision as he drives along in a steady sequence of chords that build with a patient sense of inevitability.

We're already seven minutes in and over half way through before Coltrane returns with the theme to begin his solo, flitting around the higher register like a small bird, as the rest of the band holds everything down nice and tight. He seems to settle with them for a moment before taking another short flight, returning with the theme and exploring the chords a little closer. He spins around and around as the rhythm section continues the forward momentum until they gather together for a final relaxed trawl through the tune as it slips gently away before hitting a final crescendo.

Yet this is not even generally hailed as Coltrane's masterwork. That accolade is often reserved for the 1964 recording A Love Supreme – a suite of music in four sections dedicated to God in all his forms. The truth is that for those who follow the path of Coltrane it's as close to divine as music can get. This is the sacred gospel above all others at the Church of Saint John Coltrane. And it delivers for many of us, where the Bible left us cold.

When he had completed the composition after several days locked away, he famously declared to his wife Alice that for the first time he had everything in its place. And that is exactly how it feels – the parts come together into a single whole. The recording took place four years after My Favourite

Things – several lifetimes in the development of Coltrane's music. Many jazz fans were left behind along the way.

A Love Supreme begins with Coltrane playing what it is practically a fanfare in E minor. This time he's playing tenor rather than soprano. He explores a brief solo before switching to F minor to bring in the simple riff that is the tune, adding his own voice with the repeated mantra – "A Love Supreme, A Love Supreme, A Love Supreme..."

We fly through the middle sections with plenty of space available for fine solos from Elvin Jones on drums, McCoy Tyner on piano and Jimmy Garrison on bass. Coltrane's little birds from My Favourite Things have grown into giant flying beasts as they sweep through his solo in huge movements, scooping us up and pulling us along on an irresistible journey.

The final movement Psalm is an utterly majestic and highly spiritual experiment in which Coltrane simply plays his way through a prayer, selecting notes on his saxophone for each word of a dedication to the universal spirit. If you're looking for a spiritual guide through music then they don't come any better than John Coltrane.

***

I don't actually recall the precise moment when I decided it would be OK to take a step towards the front of the church. To be honest it was more of a shuffle as the microphone was optimistically nudged towards me. But whatever the mechanics may have been, I found myself starting to blow. And for the first time in my short career as a sax player, I was soloing in front of a band – and an audience of sorts.

I had only managed to pick up a very vague notion of scales by that time with just the haziest idea of which notes might work in a given situation. And I had absolutely no idea what kind of musical situation I was in. It really was a matter of just blowing and hoping for the best. Remarkably enough, something seemed to click. Not only was I enjoying myself but the rest of the band and the whole congregation seemed to be in the same groove, dancing and hopping around in time. The music spiralled onwards and upwards.

In such a firmly spiritual context I might have been forgiven for believing the solo had been heaven-sent. If only music were that easy. But the truth is that I simply managed to take a step beyond the self-conscious – unconcerned at how bad I might sound. That's a pretty important step to take.

Whatever we might be doing, there are moments in life when we act with comparative ease – be that in a creative, intellectual or social context. The process is always a mystery to us but once we abandon ourselves to the moment with complete focus then we can somehow conjure up a little bit of magic. It's the magic of being in the moment and the magic of suspending all those negative self-critical thoughts that plague most of our lives. It's a moment that could be defined as mindfulness.

And this was just such a moment. It came on me in an irresistible wave; I have no idea how long it even lasted; in the end it simply flowed away and I sat back down – elated at sharing the moment. While it lasted I was in the flow, not thinking about notes, just feeling and going with the mood. It was like flying; like diving into the ocean and swimming with dolphins; like running through long grass with the wind in your face as music flows all around you.

Perhaps that sounds a touch self-indulgent. But I guarantee it was an extraordinarily experience and represented a significant staging post in what was still a fledgling musical journey. All very appropriate to have taken place in what has been a remarkable church ever since its inspiration back on 18 September 1965 – Franzo and Marina King's first wedding anniversary. The couple celebrated by going to San Francisco's Jazz Workshop to see Coltrane perform. They realised they would never be the same again and immediately set out to share the spiritual message they had received that night

"He lifted his soprano sax, pointed it at us, focused on us with his big clear eyes and began playing what seemed to be a non-stop one-movement suite. We did not talk to each other during the performance because we were caught up in what later would be known as our Sound Baptism. Even in a jazz club we experienced the effectual transference of the Holy Ghost through sound."

Many of us have experienced something similar – be it via Beethoven, Stravinsky, the Rolling Stones, John Coltrane or the Sex Pistols. I hadn't quite thought of it as a Sound Baptism before. But there is no doubt there is something uniquely spiritual about great music just as there is in great poetry, art or architecture – which is perhaps why all arts have been used to glorify a wide range of supreme beings throughout human history.

I'd experienced plenty of such WOW moments over a lifetime of remarkable live concerts – and even a fair few that could claim some kind of directly spiritual resonance. I particularly recall being enthralled by the choir on a visit to a Harlem church in New York, Maori chanting filling the churches every Sunday morning on a Pacific island, the sound of chanting

Monks filtering across the Mekong at dawn, the Sikh temple in Delhi that left me speechless. Devotional music is truly powerful and I was now starting to realise that all music can be devotional in its way. We are all capable of being inspired by it to reach beyond.

But as an immediate antidote to such increasingly pretentious thoughts all I had to do was remember that back in 1965 when Franzo and Marina were enjoying their date at a Coltrane gig, the next big thing on my own musical horizon was the TV pop of the Monkees. It took another five years to unearth Coltrane and 50 to finally have the guts to get up and play along.

If I wasn't already feeling like a late starter then I certainly did by the end of the performance/service when I turned to congratulate the powerhouse drummer who had kept the whole band so perfectly on track for the past two hours. I couldn't quite believe someone who looked so young as Carl could be such a brilliant musician. So I asked him.

"How long have you been playing?"

"Thirteen years."

I looked at him in disbelief as he stared back oh so seriously.

"So how old are you?"

"Fourteen years."

A big smile flashed across his impish face.

What a thrill to see a kid so on top of his art at such a young age. I started playing guitar when I was 13 but was still plodding through The Shadows' anthem Apache and Bert Weedon's Play In A Day when I was Carl's age. Play in a day? I struggled to make sense of it all my life.

And that's pretty much the point of this crazy challenge. I didn't manage it back then, so why not have a go now? Granted, it makes a lot more sense to wrestle with the intricacies of musical theory when you've got a youthful set of brain cells to play with and a whole lifetime ahead of you. But is it ever too late to play for the sheer joy of it? And maybe the process could be so much more enjoyable once the pressure of success and failure has been taken away. Once you're old enough, nobody cares how good a student you might be. That turns out to be the best time to kick back, relax and have a go.

Now the easy option would have been to go back to the guitar – I still have one in the cupboard gathering dust and I did dedicate a fair bit of time to trying to play in my youth. But if I'm to be honest, I never did learn to play. I just learned how to sound OK without getting my head around any of the hard stuff. What I wanted was to make a fresh start with an instrument that would also teach me something about music. And for some reason the soprano sax had always cast a spell over me.

First and most importantly there was Coltrane's My Favourite Things. For me that would be side one, track one of any compilation of the greatest music of all time. Back when we used to take records to parties to share our favourite discoveries, I had a Coltrane compilation that I used to take along. There were one or two reluctant admirers but it mostly got tossed to one side into a pile of ash in favour of David Bowie, Deep Purple or the current flavour of the month.

By then I'd already read the famous quote about Coltrane playing sheets of sound – a term coined in 1958 by Down Beat magazine jazz critic Ira Gitler.

"As he learned harmonically from Miles Davis and Thelonious Monk and developed his mechanical skills, a new more confident Coltrane emerged. He has used long lines and multi-noted figures within these lines but in 1958 he started playing sections that might be termed sheets of sound."

Once I had come across the idea, I decided it would be so cool to apply it to my guitar playing. Unfortunately, I couldn't be bothered with actually learning the magical notes Coltrane had assembled. It seemed good enough just to play any notes as quickly as possible. So that's what I did – to reasonable effect. It didn't teach me anything at all about music – but did have the desired effect at the time of impressing a few girls. The foundations of my school band were none too substantial and it wasn't long before we began to sink under the weight of our collective precociousness.

It was around this time that I found myself on a one-off date. Being a cheapskate I took her to a free jazz gig in an abandoned warehouse in what many years later would become London's upmarket dockside district. In the 1970s it was far from upmarket. Apart from not getting a second date, the only thing I clearly recall was the brilliant soprano sax player. I have no idea who he was but once again I was blown away. I've seen a lot of great soprano players live over the years but none that had quite the same lasting impact.

Not long after that any aspirations I had to become a rock star faded away in the face of the real world. It's from this same junction in life that I can trace my fascination with the soprano sax. Buried it may have been but through all that followed the germ of an idea continued to noodle around my mind – one day, I would learn to play the soprano.

But then in a flash 40 years had passed and incredibly I was already approaching my sixtieth birthday. I'd casually mentioned the idea to my wife Angela who took up the theme and started to encourage me. Left to my own devices I probably wouldn't have done anything about it. But now there was someone pushing me to follow a dream – daring me to put up or shut up.

If not now then when? I had no alternative but to jump in with both feet.

The general plan for my sixtieth year had already been taking shape. Angela had decided she would stop working full-time and study to become a yoga teacher. Now I come to think of it, her encouragement for me to take up the soprano was pretty modest in comparison – but it was an effective sweetener and a great idea. I had agreed.

Seeing as how most of my recent work had been escorting tour groups around the world, we were able to put together an itinerary for Angela's first year of freedom and my sixtieth year that took in two to three months each in Sicily, the USA and Cambodia – as well as a little time back home in Brighton.

I was at a crossroads – looking back on the first 60 years of life and looking forward to what remained. And I have to say I was looking forward to it with enthusiasm having discovered the truth in reports that old age can be the happiest time of your life. And the first year at least was all set to be a blast – with trips to three of my favourite places on Earth. With a soprano sax for company I could really start to explore the truth of My Favourite Things.

But now I'd also have to squeeze in some music lessons and some hard graft. It wasn't going to be easy. One thing was for sure though – there was no way this would be a casual affair. I was determined that within a year I would approach some kind of proficiency and within two I'd be playing my first gig.

I wasn't sure it would be quite so easy to measure the success of our new lives together but I had a hunch the key would be in the diverse threads of the journey ahead – travel, music and yoga. The Zen of sax.

# CHAPTER TWO

## Music Is Seriously Good For Your Health – Play Your Way to Wellbeing

So why would anyone decide to take up a musical instrument later in life? Surely the moment has passed?

You know what? The question makes a lot more sense the other way round. Why would anyone not decide to open up their life to the sheer joy and incredible benefits of music making? Music delivers on so many levels but disappoints on very few.

Let's start with the negative just to get the old chestnuts out of the way. I'll level with you. You're not going to sound very good for the first few weeks – or even months. You're going to worry what the neighbours think. You're going to worry what your family and friends think. You're even going to worry what the dog might think.

But you know what? It doesn't matter. So long as you're respectful to others regarding your practice hours and keep the sound to as reasonable a level as possible, nobody is going to judge you. In fact you'd be surprised at just how much encouragement you'll get along the way.

A more serious consideration for many is the idea that it takes a really long time to learn an instrument – and it gets harder to learn the older you get. Now these points are worthy of consideration.

The bottom line is that it can take a long time if you want to get really good at anything. According to the much-quoted Malcolm Gladwell in Outliers: The Story Of Success, that can actually be quantified. In order to fully master any skill from music to football to computer programming to oil painting, he reckons you need to put in around 10,000 hours. And there is a certain amount of research to back that up.

Now that works out at more than two hours of every day for 15 years. If you don't play every single day or you put in less than two hours at a time it could be as much as 20 or 30 years. Gladwell himself seems to recommend 20 hours a week for 10 years. If you're a teenager, that might not seem such a problem. But later in life you may well have the sense that you're running out of time. And couldn't all those hours be better spent playing golf or just relaxing over a glass of wine?

The truth of course is that if golf is what turns you on then go for it. If playing the saxophone or the guitar is your thing then equally a couple of hours a day devoted to pursuing your pleasure can offer a pretty good return. And there's always time for that glass of wine when you're done. It's all about balance.

And who said anything about becoming a fluent musician? If 10,000 hours is what it takes to master a skill then how many does it take to learn enough just to have fun? From my own experience the answer to that is pretty close to zero. So long as you engage in enjoying the process for its own sake, it'll start rewarding you from day one. There's only ever going to be a problem if you choose to compare yourself as you are with a fictitious self you believe you should be. And that's a dangerous road to follow.

Whatever your stage of life, it's so important to engage fully in the moment. We all know this intuitively but it's a lot easier said than done. The young can have an eye to the future with some justification – even though the joy of youth is all about living for today.

That's something we tend to lose sight of as we progress through our middle years, getting swamped by the tough stuff of life and all too often becoming progressively more miserable. But the older we get the more important the now becomes all over again – there's no need to plan things anymore. And you know what? That makes life so much richer, more enjoyable and less stressful. It's why all the studies show that we tend to reach a happiness low point in middle age and then start to pick up again to a new high as we continue to age.

And it's regaining the sense of now that gives us a second chance. So far as I can make out, the two best times in life to learn an instrument are when you are young or when you are old. Of course we don't actually call 60 old anymore – but you know what I mean.

Indeed the idea of running out of time no longer applies in anything like the same way it once did, with most of us living significantly longer and more active lives. There's still plenty of time in our golden years to take up an instrument – or return to one that might have been abandoned long ago.

The bottom line at all times is to remember: music is fun. That's the mantra. It's what you have to bear in mind when all you want to do is scream in desperation because your practice session is not going to plan. It's all too hard. I'm not good enough. I simply can't do this.

So if that's where you find yourself, don't do it. Just walk away and tell yourself: music is fun – I can do this. But I'll do it another day. And I am good enough – I just don't feel like it right now.

Whether or not we have ever played a musical instrument, most of us can enjoy music at some level or another. We may have different tastes but when it hits the spot its effects can be absolutely electric. It can energise us; it can relax us; it can alter our mood; it can transport us through space and time. If it's a piece we've heard before, then all it might take is a single chord to instantly resonate with our past selves. There is no faster or more powerful way to travel through time and connect with distant memories.

Partly for these reasons it's also incredibly good for our physical and mental wellbeing. Ancient cultures all over the planet have long integrated music into healing ceremonies and rituals and western therapists now also use it for a wide range of therapeutic applications.

Clearly, music offers a link between our mental, emotional, spiritual and physical selves. And those same notes which effortlessly transport us between sadness and joy or from the present day to many years ago are no more than physical sensations. They are sound waves that have been created on an instrument by some physical means, transmitted through particles of air, vibrating our eardrums, moving the small bones behind them, passing on that tiny movement to a fluid within the inner ear and finally onto hair cells which transmit an electrical charge along our auditory nerve.

And that's not even the end of the story. There's then a whole sequence of refinements, which combine all the available information and present the entire package to the cortex of our brain. Only then can the information be interpreted. And you know what? That particular area of the brain turns out to be larger among musicians. It's just like weightlifting expanding our muscles.

The brain provides all kinds of magic for us all – musicians or not. Music can trigger areas of the brain that are also activated by other stimulants such as food and sex. All of them can result in the release of dopamine – a natural high at the most pleasurable moments of a musical experience.

The incredible journey that music takes through our brains without us even being conscious of it makes for powerful therapeutic applications for patients who cannot be reached in other ways. Even those with advanced dementia can easily recall and enjoy music from the distant past. It can be a powerful tool when working with the whole range of learning disabilities and there's also evidence that music may even be able to reach those locked into a coma.

It's health benefits can reach almost everyone with effects such as lowering blood pressure and pulse rate through to pain relief. These effects may result from being fully immersed in an activity – there are similar claims for meditation or chanting. Indeed, listening to music is much akin to meditation and can have a deeply spiritual dimension – just witness how many religious or spiritual ceremonies throughout the world involve some kind of music or chanting.

But if you don't enjoy the activity – or a particular form of music – then clearly the magic is not going to work. I can't say rap or even a lot of contemporary pop does much to lower my blood pressure. And I'm sure that a lot of people would say the same about a lengthy free-form John Coltrane sax solo.

But when it does work it can do so to remarkable effect. Studies of peak experiences reveal frequent reports of heightened emotional responses and a sense of physically dissolving into the music. Such events can lead us to feel we have gained new insights and this is a fundamental part of music's power. It doesn't need words to communicate – we feel what it has to say.

There have been various studies into the idea of Flow among musicians – even among heavy metal bands. The concept of optimal functioning while performing an activity allows us to focus on the transcendental nature of live performance. The experience can take musicians beyond conscious thought to merge with one another and the audience into what can only be described as a single ritual event. Awareness merges into the action with a loss of self-awareness and a distorted perception of time. The participant perceives optimum achievement and enjoyment through being totally engaged in the process.

This is something that can also often be combined with movement. Many of us will have experienced almost ecstatic moments while gyrating on the dance floor. Quite possibly this may have been linked with a liberal consumption of alcohol and a certain degree of sexual stimulus. But music is also an essential dimension in the experience. Just as it is within mystical experiences such as Sufism, Native American war dancing, shamanistic rituals and even modern western club culture.

So if the benefits of music itself are so all pervasive, what are the specific benefits of playing a musical instrument? And how do these come into their own for an older age profile?

Apart from any physical effects of blowing, plucking or striking an instrument and the social gain of sharing the activity with others, there are huge benefits for the health of your brain. Use it or lose it is the old saying. And this turns out to be spot on.

There is little doubt that the more new connections we can forge in our brains, then the healthier we will be – and the better protected we are against its deterioration. Learning any new skill can be helpful. Personally, I was learning Italian at the same time as I started playing the sax and language acquisition is another winner in this respect. So I'm hoping I've now doubled my chances!

Playing music is particularly helpful in that it's all about forging new connections between different parts of the brain. It has actually been established that this activity changes its very structure – the bundle of nerve fibres that connect the left and right sides of the brain are thicker among those who have undergone musical training. This is possibly because music draws on such a wide range of different skills that require co-ordinated attention from different zones of the brain – pitch recognition, timing and rhythm, movement of parts of the body, sight-reading, interpretation of a structure, memory, collaborative working, emotional expression and so on.

Playing any form of music requires all of these skills and provides similar benefits. It's possible to make claims for different approaches. It could be argued for example that classical training is more rigorous, blues or soul more emotional, folk more intimate. My own speciality is jazz and that brings a major element of improvisation – and yet another set of challenges.

The brains of jazz musicians have been studied in an MRI scanner while they improvise. It was found that the parts devoted to self-monitoring actually closed down, allowing the brain to focus unimpeded on the process.

And it is quite a feat. Firstly, it requires memorising and internalising an incredible number of rules and exceptions to rules from a study of jazz theory, familiarity with a whole canon of musical history and mastery of an instrument. Then all of that information needs to be pushed into the background as the musician listens to and watches the rest of the band, playing appropriately to what is heard – and creating an original performance. On top of that the whole thing will hopefully turn out to be both interesting and expressive.

All I can say is, if my brain can manage that lot then it's getting a pretty good workout. And just like our physical bodies, the more exercise it gets then the better that bodes for the future.

Then there is all the psychological evidence that playing music actually makes us happier people. There is of course the exception of certain well-documented professionals whose lifestyle leads them into a life of drug and alcohol dependency and consequent depression and even mental illness. But it could well be argued that these are people who would be prone to such a lifestyle anyway and it may not be the process of playing an instrument itself that leads them down the slippery slope.

While writing this book, I took part in a psychological study looking into the impact of playing a musical instrument or singing on wellbeing among both professional and amateur musicians. Results consistently showed that it took just 20 minutes of playing for the whole range of participants to experience increased feelings of joy, happiness, carefreeness and contentment.

The truth is that there's a lot of fun to be had in making a glorious noise. That's the case at every level – and perhaps even more so for the non-professional with none of the pressures that go with that world. It's also a very sociable hobby and the rewards of playing increase exponentially once you start sharing the experience with others.

And you'd be surprised at just how many mature music students there are out there. Once you make a start and reach out for a local network you'll find there's no shortage of people who share your passion.

Go for it!

# CHAPTER THREE

## Back To School
## – Musical Beginnings

So where did it all begin – this lifelong obsession with popular music? I put it down to simply being a child of my time. Like others born in the 50s, growing up in the 60s and coming into our own in the 70s, our formative years were a road map for an emerging youth culture and the soundtrack that was beating at its heart. Music came from nowhere and suddenly was everywhere – it led a revolution, it was in our blood.

I was born in Chelmsford – a small boring town much like all the small boring towns in England at that time. There was no music at home – no piano or record player. Yet there was always a sense that somewhere out there something was going on. Unfortunately there was little direct evidence of it – just rumours. We didn't have a TV for most of my early school years and BBC radio was a desert so far as our generation was concerned.

Then one Christmas the outside world suddenly arrived in our living room in the shape of a Dansette record player together with the latest Beatles singles – a present for my older brother Ed. But it changed my world just as much, the lights turning on in our lives with a new energy that shook up our dull lives. She Loves You, I Wanna Hold Your Hand, Twist and Shout, Long Tall Sally. Rock and Roll had arrived in Rectory Lane and there was no turning back.

It didn't take long for all the trappings of pop music to enter our lives. Out went kids stuff like the exploits of Dan Dare in the Eagle. Now it was time to switch from comics to music weeklies to find the best new singles. Along came Record Mirror, Disc, Melody Maker and NME. Reading about music was almost exciting as hearing it.

And to actually hear it was an adventure in itself. The only place for that was Dace's – a dusty old musical instrument shop that also sold records. But how did you know you would like something when you had never heard it before? If it was any good, the BBC certainly wouldn't have played it.

The earliest solution was the record booth – a hangover from the days when record collectors were serious people who knew how to take good care of delicate vinyl. That was no longer the case as parties of rowdy youths gathered in a series of little rooms, each with its own record player, a pile of singles in their grubby hands, ready to give them a spin. It was a thrilling moment of decision, surrounded by the intoxicating aroma of vinyl and stale tobacco. Do I blow three weeks' pocket money on this or not?

But the biggest problem of all was to decide who would be my favourite band. There was no way it could be the Beatles – Ed was already collecting their records and the whole point of pop was to be different. I toyed with the Dave Clark Five for a while and was always ready to be charmed by a female singer like Dusty Springfield.

Then came the day when the lost was found and I became a true believer in positive thinking. It was also the day I decided all my uncertainties could be resolved if I were to buy a Rolling Stones record and declare them to be my new favourite band. Their latest release was The Last Time so I headed into town with a ten bob note (50p) in my pocket.

After a spin around Woolworths to pick up a quarter of lemon sherbets, I was on my way to Dace's.

As ever, I would take my time. There was no point in rushing the pleasure of such a purchase. Into the shop, with a ring of the bell as it closed behind me, past the boring instruments and sheet music and up the stairs to where the real action was. Emerging on the first floor, it was time to breathe it all in, with a glance around at the posters for live events at the Corn Exchange that I could only dream of, a browse through the LP section I couldn't afford, a careful examination of this week's charts to see if there was anything I had missed in Record Mirror. Finally I could approach the counter.

"The Last Time by the Rolling Stones," I said – trying to give the impression I bought their records all the time. "Can I listen to it first please?"

As if I'd ever buy a record without the pleasure of taking it into the listening booth for the thrill of indecision. But as soon as that opening guitar hook crashed in I knew I couldn't back out. This was the record that could finally make me cool. I'd be a Rolling Stones fan. Might as well play it again though, just to get full value from the experience.

I finally slipped the record back into its sleeve and stuffed a hand into my pocket. Disaster! It can't be! It was empty. I broke into a cold sweat. I'd lost my money and it would take weeks to save up again. And by then The Last Time wouldn't be cool anymore! What on Earth could I do? I was lost in a daze until a brisk tap of irritation on the glass door brought me back to reality. I had to go. And worst of all, I had to hand over my passport to cool.

"No thank you," I muttered – looking down at my shoes, convinced the eyes of the whole shop were on this pathetic kid who didn't like the Rolling Stones.

I was close to tears. But by the time I was down the stairs and out the front door, I had a plan. I would retrace my steps, taking precisely the same route through town that I had taken an hour before. Who knows? Perhaps I would find my 10 shillings, still be able to buy The Last Time and nobody need ever know I wasn't a Stones fan after all.

So that's what I did, working my way around Chelmsford like a latter-day Ulysses until I arrived back at the loose sweets counter in Woolworths. I looked down on the floor just in front of the lemon sherbets and my heart leapt. There it was – a 10-shilling note. My note. And nobody had seen it for the past hour. If this wasn't divine providence I didn't know what was.

I made sure nobody was watching as I scooped it up and hurried back to Dace's – filled with a warm glow. That was the day I learned to trust destiny. Some things are simply meant to be. It was the power of belief, the power of music. Right then that record was more important than anything in my world.

\*\*\*

Until I was 13 I shared a bedroom with my brother. There was one big consolation for the lack of space – his love of offshore pirate radio stations. In later years he actually worked on-board the Radio Caroline ship. But back in the early 60s the highlight of the day was snuggling up under the covers as he tuned into the Johnnie Walker show, introducing us to the wonderful world of soul music – the unbelievable black American sounds that were still largely ignored by mainstream media and may as well not have existed at all so far as white America was concerned. It was a significant sub-set of the musical revolution already underway – but a revolution you could dance to.

This was the world of Otis Redding, Aretha Franklin, Wilson Picket, Sam and Dave, Booker T and the MGs – a host of great performers who only began to break through American racial barriers after they had already become stars in Europe. And that breakthrough was largely down to being played by the pirate radio stations – paving the way for a big tour in

1967 when they were stunned to discover how popular they had become outside their own country.

The pirate stations – especially Radio Caroline and Radio London – were the big game changers for us all. Denied any reasonable musical offerings by a BBC still mired in post-war greyness and only able to access the rare light of Radio Luxembourg through late-night static, it was down to the pirates to break down the walls and allow a sense of what was waiting for us out there.

But they only had a short legal lifespan – three years from their arrival until legislation was passed to ban them – with only Caroline surviving as an outlaw operator. If there was to be a plus from this it was the recognition by the BBC that it had not been serving the nation's musical needs. And so Radio One was born – largely staffed by DJs recruited from the old offshore stations. And while the daytime was packed with pop from the singles charts, an occasional night time slot was found for Radio London refugee John Peel – who had originally learned his craft on American FM stations.

Top Gear and Night Ride were more than just primers in the new 'alternative' or 'Underground' music that had been sweeping live venues (frustratingly still inaccessible to a young schoolboy). While Peel would include the earliest offerings from Pink Floyd, Cream and Jefferson Airplane, it was the addition of field recordings of blues musicians from the Mississippi Delta, poetry marathons, experimental electronic music and slabs of far out avant-garde jazz that opened the minds of a generation.

I could sense a whole new world out there on the horizon in shimmering Technicolor – like the moment when Dorothy leaves grey old Kansas behind and drops into the wonderful world of Oz.

School was part of the dust-heap of the old world while my education had moved on to the NME, Rolling Stone and International Times, listening to Top Gear and spending Saturday afternoons listening to the latest imports at Pop Inn – a new shop that had blown Dace's out the water with its progressive music policy and modern kiosks to listen to a whole album at a time.

This was also the time I discovered the incredible resource that was the town's record library. If I could go back in time, one of my first stops would be to track down and shake the curator by the hand to thank him or her from the bottom of my heart for the incredible collection they had put together. And so far as I could make out, it was all for me.

## THE JOY OF SAX

There was a large well-used classical department. And I would sift through it from time to time to educate myself with works by Stravinsky, Prokofiev, Shostokovitch, Stockhausen, Messiaen, Riley and so on. But then there was my private section, featuring an incredible primer to the very best examples from the history of folk, blues and jazz. I worked my way through the lot over the years and ended up making many new friends along the way – from Louis Armstrong to Duke Ellington to Lester Young to Charlie Parker to Miles Davis to John Coltrane and every stop in between.

\*\*\*

This was a real education – unlike school, which always seemed to look backwards rather than forwards, always a chore rather than a revelation. Music lessons were the realm of Miss Grant – a dragon with a ruler at the ready to wrap you over the knuckles should you dare hit a white note instead of a black one. Even touching a piano was a rarity as we were mostly restricted to hieroglyphics on the board, only making any sense to those who had already grown up with music. To the rest of us they might as well have been Mandarin.

When I first arrived at secondary school we had been offered the opportunity to learn an instrument. I opted for the trumpet.

I'm not sure I had a good reason apart from the fact it seemed reasonably portable.

When I turned up for my first lesson I was told that all the trumpets had all gone and that I'd have to settle for a trombone. I groaned at the thought of having to lug such a huge thing all the way to school and back. I stuck with it for 30 minutes, even managing a few farty noises in the mouthpiece. But I never went back. My musical career was going nowhere.

It was when I was 13, with the benefit of my extra-curricular crash course in 20$^{th}$ century culture that things started to change. The precise moment was the first day of term, when a teacher asked a new classmate about an elder brother who had since left the school.

The classroom was permanent chaos whenever a liberal teacher was on board, ink-soaked pellets of blotting paper flying across the room, initials being carved on desk lids and occasional bursts of laughter as the class clown did his impression of the head. But I was all-ears, craning forwards to follow the conversation, which had taken a particularly interesting turn.

Jerry hopped from foot to foot and gazed out of the window as the teacher awaited his reply.

"Well, at the moment he's working with a pop group called The Doors," he muttered, desperate to get out of the spotlight and back behind his desk.

"Do give Tony my regards, won't you?" came the beaming reply.

My eyes were glued to Jerry in admiration as he shuffled past. The Doors! Wow! His brother works with The Doors! I couldn't wait to grab him when break time came round.

"I overheard what you just said – about your brother working for The Doors."

He looked at me blankly.

"Why? Have you heard of them then?"

"You're kidding. The Doors – Light My Fire – they're amazing! What's you're brother do?"

"He's organising stuff for them at the Roundhouse this week."

"You mean they're in England? Right now?"

"Suppose so. And next month he's doing Blue Cheer. Normally he does the live tours for Soft Machine. You heard of them?"

"All of them! Wow!"

And so a new friendship began with two 13-year-olds skating around the fringes of London's alternative music scene – following the exploits of Tony's more obscure but super-cool band of revolutionaries Mick Farren's Social Deviants and, of course, everything involving the Soft Machine family.

But most important of all, we both decided to start learning the guitar. There were no lessons available on such a blatantly anti-establishment instrument. The last thing the school (which had pretensions above its station) wanted to encourage was the development of delinquent beat groups.

So we both saved for a guitar, invested in copies of Bert Weedon's celebrated Play In A Day and hit the trail of bleeding fingers and out of tune Apache marathons. Jerry was a natural. Or perhaps he just worked harder. I never seemed to get anywhere – although I realised later that this was probably because I only ever bothered with one major scale and a handful of chords before I settled for posing in front of the mirror.

But even with a limited musical vocabulary, there were some big pluses. Number one was the ability to avoid the playground at break times – I'd never understood the attraction of running around in the freezing cold only to be smashed to the ground by a posse of oversized bullies. Instead we used to take refuge in the music rooms.

It didn't take long to upgrade to a second-hand electric guitar and amplifier. I still couldn't play – but now it was loud and distorted! Every so often I tried playing with another friend who had an electric organ. But he was far too good and there was a permanent look of disappointment on his face.

I eventually managed to start creeping out to live music venues. When I was 15 I made it to one of the earliest open-air festivals – featuring the likes of Led Zeppelin, Pink Floyd, Jefferson Airplane, Santana and the Byrds. My musical education was rounding out nicely.

Jerry and I continued playing together and attempted to write a few tunes – Jerry's always more successful than my own. Our first and only gig as a duo was an impromptu event at the local girls' school. It may not have been a musical triumph but it did open our eyes to our guitars' potential for stirring female hormones.

Any lack in technique was more than made up for by enthusiasm and we decided to start a band together with a bass player and drummer from the year below. It was a time when endless noodling on a riff could pass for music. For some bizarre reason we decided to make Soft Machine's fiendishly complex Facelift our signature tune, padded it out with 20 minutes of random notes, added in a few odd scraps of our own and rounded it off with a couple of rock and roll instrumentals. We didn't own a microphone and none of us could sing anyway so the whole thing was pretty much an endless guitar riff.

After a few rehearsals we declared ourselves ready and put ourselves forward as support act at the school dance. We had the home crowd on our side so it seemed to go down pretty well. I developed my simplified variation on Coltrane's sheets of sound – fast is good. I was going to be a rock star!

Buoyed by our success we were booked to a local club. Just beforehand the drummer (who was good enough to know he was indispensible) fell out with the bass player and insisted we sack him. I switched to bass and we stumbled through our second and final gig. My career was over!

A few months later we left school and lost touch. I took some wrong turns and before I knew it was stuck in the middle of my first failed marriage. I eventually gathered myself together having left all musical dreams behind and sailed through a second, longer but also ultimately doomed marriage.

I consciously hoped to do things differently after that, treating myself to spells of healing through travel, meditation and psychoanalysis. But there was still something missing. I knew there was an answer waiting out there but I was still groping in the dark for the lost chord.

# CHAPTER FOUR

## A Taste For Travel
## – Setting The Stage

Out of the road crash of a second divorce, I still didn't turn to music for salvation. As we all know, logic doesn't come into it when you're on the floor. There are however a few clear phases we often weave our way through while seeking a new equilibrium.

We treat ourselves to a new toy, a favourite meal, a nice bottle of wine – just beware the fine line of self-destructive bouts of depression marked by excessive consumption. Then there's freedom – the most natural response to separation – the feeling that you're free to go wherever you want, whenever you want to go. And there's no doubt travel is a powerful healer – particularly if you're prepared to shed an old skin and engage with the new.

But freedom is a difficult monster to wrestle and for some it's a step too far. Freedom to travel can easily mutate into loneliness – or just fear of loneliness. Travel works its magic best as a chance to share, explore and learn – not watching from the sidelines. Otherwise it can do more harm than good.

But travel was in my blood. It had always been a default position so far as I was concerned. My mother used to say it was because I was born on a Thursday – Thursday's child has far to go...

So I really had no choice in the matter and took time out for two lengthy trips to South East Asia – a region I'd not previously explored. They were a revelation. Everything I could have hoped for – a new life, new friends, new experiences – everything necessary for at least an illusion of a new self.

One of my most valued companions was the Italian writer Tiziano Terzani and his book A Fortune-Teller Told Me. While based in the Far East as a foreign correspondent, a fortune-teller had predicted that if he were to fly during the course of a particular year he would die. He therefore resolved to travel only by land and sea for 12 months and the book was a record of his experience. It's a wonderful insight into a true traveller in search of enlightenment.

I was impressed enough to follow in his footsteps by consulting a fortune-teller at a Bangkok temple – in the peaceful grounds of beautiful Wat Pho – and found myself equally impressed by Mr Chang's uncannily accurate assessment of my life so far. After noting down details of the date, place and time of my birth, he disappeared into a trance of intense calculations with columns of numbers rapidly filling a school exercise book. Then he grabbed my hand and studied it with great interest for several minutes before completing his calculations with a satisfied smile.

He looked up and spoke – in Chinese. I looked in turn at the interpreter sitting by his side.

"Mr Chang, he says you are creative person – a writer – and that you have own business – maybe two. You have had marriage end twice and have one children. "

All this was spot on. He had my attention.

"You like travel but make decisions too fast. Need to slow down. You very good at what you do. You a strong person who can get others to do what you want. You are charming man and so can have many partners."

A little bit of flattery always gets you a long way in my book. Sounded good to me. He went on to go through the years of my life to date, setting out good times and bad ones with a fair degree of accuracy, going on to do the same for the future with warnings for certain periods to beware of health problems.

"A new partner should not be from your own country. Should be someone very different from you. Should be slim – but not too slim. Should be beautiful and should certainly wear white."

Mr Chang set me up nicely for the journey ahead – with his successful recipe of inspired intuition, combined with a flattering assessment and an intriguing peep into the future. Two journeys through Thailand, Laos and Cambodia taught me a lot about myself, other people I encountered and a history and tragic legacy that hangs like a smoke that never clears.

So far as my own journey was concerned, the next phase was the personal challenge to be undertaken. This is what could be described in mythic terms as the search for the Holy Grail and it turns out to be another common and useful part of the post-separation toolkit.

A tough journey through the more remote parts of South-East Asia could provide just such a test. But as I had undergone a fair bit of adventurous travel over the years, it was perhaps no longer quite the challenge it once was. So I returned to the UK and Ireland (where I had previously been based) and vowed to follow in Terzani's footsteps – no air travel for a year. It seemed the process of grounding myself might be a tough but necessary step towards literally getting my feet back on the ground. I explored a few courses in yoga and meditation and took time out to take stock when my father died.

Whilst I wasn't consciously looking for something to challenge myself, it's the only way I can retrospectively make sense of my next utterly bizarre step, choosing to go to a drama school and sign up for an intensive acting course.

Now for some people that might have been the fulfilment of a life-long ambition. Fair enough. But I could never recall ever having wanted to act. In fact as a child, the very idea of going on stage had filled me with dread. I always had an appalling memory so learning lines was a chore I had always failed. I knew that if I were to volunteer for a part in a play I would be dumbstruck with fear at the prospect of forgetting every word – let alone looking like a complete idiot. It simply wasn't for me.

It never even occurred to me to pick up on music again. That might have made some kind of sense – to continue where I had left off, following my passion, doing something I knew I loved. But maybe that wasn't the point. Perhaps I needed to pursue something impossible – something I couldn't do. That's the only way I can understand such scrambled logic.

The truth is that it turned out to be an incredibly useful process – as would any shared experience with a group of motivated individuals. But it was clear from Day One that everyone else in the class was desperate to become an actor. I was there for self-improvement.

And you know what? Most of the early bits at drama schools are taken up with exercises – the stuff you do when you're not actually learning lines or performing. And most of those exercises are all about personal growth – simply becoming a better person. Despite what many of us may think, acting turns out to be about finding yourself – not about pretending to be someone you're not. That's just the way to bad acting and an empty life.

So drama school turned out to be a good idea after all – just so long as I didn't get too carried away with the idea of becoming an actor. All the old fears were still there – even if I had learned to keep them under control. So after putting myself through three terms and against all the odds managing to learn enough lines for three plays, I decided to call it quits. I had taken what I could from the process and was ready to move on.

Shortly afterwards I was invited to a party. As soon as I arrived I saw two friends talking to a woman I didn't know. I began chatting to them without realising the stranger was now behind me, totally excluded from the conversation. I turned to apologise and stopped dead in my tracks. She was beautiful, dressed all in white, slim but not too slim. And when she spoke I realised that she wasn't English – not from my own country. Thank you Mr Chang.

I spent the rest of the evening talking to Angela, her home in Italy and all the things we seemed to have in common. The following weekend we went on our first date – a walk in the countryside – and have been together ever since.

We had both been through our share of darkness, had both experienced the pain when things go wrong. But we had also both taken time to look into ourselves and find some kind of renewal before falling into a new love.

One of the most refreshing things from the outset was that no demands were ever placed on either of us and there was a level of encouragement I had never experienced before.

Within a matter of weeks we were travelling together in Italy and I reciprocated immediately in my own wanderlust way.

"Fancy coming to Timbuktu?"

"Are you crazy?"

"There's a Tuareg music Festival there next month. I thought it might be fun."

"OK."

So there we were sitting on a sand dune in the middle of the Sahara when she delivered her first major encouragement. By then I had written some scripts for children's TV. So I remarked on what a great setting this could be for an animated film and began to make up a story about the Blue Men of Timbuktu.

"You must do it. Don't ever have any doubt."

"But... You don't understand. It would take forever. It's too difficult."

"You can do it."

She looked at me with such certainty that I began to doubt my own doubts. It was an encouragement that launched years of effort that very nearly delivered – only the worldwide financial crash and last-minute collapse of the principal partner finally drawing a curtain over that particular dream.

But the whole process remained as a tribute to the power of positive thinking and Angela's ability to encourage me to take that extra step into the unknown. It was a role she was to play once again when it came to jump starting a musical career that had already lain dormant for 40 years.

***

I was a few months shy of my 60th birthday and the idea of impending old age was driving me to seek out new challenges. By then I was picking up work with a travel company taking tour groups to various parts of the world – especially Vietnam and Cambodia. In December, I ended a tour in Cambodia and took the short flight back to Saigon to meet Angela as she arrived from London. It was the following night at Saigon's premier jazz venue that out plan for the following year began to take shape.

Our brief stop in the bright lights of downtown and a few days at the beach were a soft landing in preparation for a trip up to the Highlands. We were on our way to Dalat for a yoga retreat. It now turned out that his was only to be a taster for a much longer yoga teacher-training course that Angela had already identified for the following year. If all went well in Vietnam (and it did) her plan was to sign up for the full package at the same guru's ashram in California.

She was already thinking about her own journey. We were only five months away from my birthday and the clock was ticking towards my Year of Sixty. When the band took a break, as usual she had a few interesting suggestions.

"Seeing as how you're going to be 60, I think I should stop working."

"But you're younger than me. You won't be 60 for ages yet."

"You mean you don't think I deserve to be a lady of leisure?"

"Well..."

"It's not the same for you. You're self-employed."

I nodded and took a sip of beer. She had a point.

"You're always saying it's a problem with me working full time because we can't make the most of your flexible lifestyle."

"True..."

"We could spend a lot more time together."

"Which is why you want to spend two months on your own in an ashram?"

"Well, I'm sure you could find something you want to do at the same time. What about that new American tour you were offered – to New Orleans. You love jazz. It would be perfect."

"OK. Sold. You know what though? Once you've qualified, we should come back to Cambodia. I want to spend more time there. It's a beautiful place –and I'm sure there'd be an opportunity for you to teach."

"Deal. But you know what? There's still something missing. It's your big birthday. You need a big project?"

"Can't I just take it easy?"

"No. It's not good for you."

She turned to look at the bandstand with a wicked smile – a smile I've come to know only too well. All I could do was signal to the waiter to bring another beer. I knew something was coming.

"You know what? It's not enough just to go to New Orleans. You ought to learn to play jazz."

"But that would take forever. It's too difficult."

I felt like I was time travelling. I'd shot straight back in time and I was sitting on top of that same sand dune in the middle of the Sahara.

"Of course you can do it. You know you've always wanted to play the soprano sax."

"I know. But..."

"If you don't do it now you never will. We'll get one for your birthday."

I've always said Angela was a witch – a very positive one of course – with an innate ability to be perfectly in tune with the moment. If evidence were ever needed, the band ambled back on stage and started playing My Favourite Things – the very tune I had yearned all my life to play on the soprano.

I'll never know if it was more than intuition. But the magic cast its spell. By the time we left the club, the plan was complete. I would look for a soprano when we got back to Brighton and take a few lessons. Angela would give in her notice and we'd organise a joint party for my birthday and her leaving work.

Then on the day of my birthday we would fly to Sicily for three months. We'd long been searching for a little bit of Italy to call our own and had finally come to the conclusion that Sicily could be the answer. So we'd promised ourselves that we would rent a place for long enough to decide if it could be a potential new home. And now I'd also have a new hobby to pursue while I was there.

We'd return to Brighton for a quick pit stop before heading to the USA for a holiday together to celebrate Angela's birthday in September. She would retire to her Ashram while I headed across country to lead a couple of tours through the Deep South, taking in a string of music capitals from Nashville to Memphis to New Orleans.

Finally, we would winter in Cambodia, combining some tour work for me with yoga teaching for Angela. And all the time I'd have a soprano saxophone for company. Now that's what I call a year to remember!

# CHAPTER FIVE

## Sax At Sixty
## – Now or Never

Angela was right of course. Jazz had been an important thread in my life – a passion that couldn't be buried. I'd loved music since the day the Beatles arrived in our living room, passing through phases of pop, rock, folk, blues, classical, Indian, African, Latin and every combination. But it was the indefinable essence that was jazz that held it all together – and had bubbled back to the surface in recent years.

Once again my old jazz records had found their way to the front of the pile, I was going to jazz festivals and concerts at every opportunity, without even realising I'd ever been away and born again into a jazz skin. It had crept up so gradually I hadn't even noticed the rebirth happening. I was still listening to and enjoying every form of music but jazz was back to the fore.

And above all it was the sheer life-affirming joy of jazz improvisation that was the key. Jazz is a pretty broad church and I have to say I'm no purist by any stretch of the imagination. In fact, the more pure or traditional it is then the more it leaves me cold. For me, music is life and only works on the level where it produces and passes on something resembling the spark of life.

In my book that means there are two distinct threads of worthwhile sounds – music for the body and music for the spirit. I'm always ready to lead the way to the dance-floor. So jazz that crosses over into rock, funk, soul, Latin or African beats are all fair game. And there's a lot of fun to be had in the sheer exuberance of the music, taking in everything from a New Orleans marching band, to Fela Kuti's sweaty Afrobeat, to Cuban Salsa or Brazilian Bossa Nova, to disco classics from Chic and everything that swings.

But then there's the more spiritual side of things – music not just for listening to but for dreaming. And my old friend John Coltrane belongs in that world. It's a rich heritage that draws on traditions from all around the planet – Coltrane even named his son Ravi after Indian sitar master Ravi Shankar. It's music to float within on a journey of discovery. At its best there's a trusting no questions asked relationship between listener and performer, allowing yourself to be taken to unexpected destinations. That's a powerful music that includes both the drifting stream of My Favourite Things and the more demanding rocky rapids of A Love Supreme.

I couldn't possibly choose between the physical and spiritual threads of the music – and of course they interact and cross-pollinate all the time. I was aware that my life of travel and adventure had also been a journey through music. But I'd been riding on a free pass for too long. It was time to dive into the deep end and try to actually play some of what I had grown to love.

I was never crazy enough to imagine that I could manage anything that even approached the sounds of my musical heroes. But I had a sense that in order to appreciate them even more – reach yet another level – then I needed to understand more. This was going to be a real journey just like all the roads I had followed around the world.

I'm pretty good at organising travel so I know where I'm heading. But I also knew that everything would change once this journey had begun and that I would hopefully learn some surprising things along the way and come back a changed person. I knew that because it had always happened that way. And why should a musical journey be different?

So it was with a spirit of adventure – like a traveller – that I decided to dive back into the ocean of music, recognising that this was an opportunity to go deeper than I had ever dreamed. I had a sense that if I applied myself to learning how to play the music with something of the spirit of my heroes then I might begin to appreciate and understand a little more of what they had been offering me.

That clearly also had a spiritual dimension. Angela would soon be heading off on a personal journey that would take her deeper into yoga and meditation in the knowledge that deepening her own practice would inevitably deepen her understanding of her guru's spiritual message. The same was true of my personal musical journey. All journeys have a lot in common and I had a clear sense that my musical route ran parallel to Angela's Ashram experience.

While there was no particular magic about doing anything at a particular age, it seemed to me that a milestone like 60 was a pretty good time to take a significant fork in the road. And Angela was right – if not now then when?

## THE JOY OF SAX

So, soon after we got back to Brighton, I checked out the local saxophone teachers. Raymond lived nearby, seemed to have plenty of experience and offered to hire out a saxophone for a six-week package so I could get a sense of whether it was for me before committing to an instrument. It seemed like a pretty good way to make a start so I booked a trial lesson.

The trial gave him an opportunity to tell me the rules on timekeeping. I was told that I would need to arrive several minutes early and wait in the hall. While there I should set up my instrument. At precisely the designated moment for my 45-minute slot, the previous student would come out and I would enter. At the end of exactly 45 minutes I would leave and another student would take my place.

He then went on to try to persuade me to give up on the idea of playing the soprano as it was supposedly the most difficult place to start in the whole saxophone family. This is indeed a familiar refrain in the sax subculture. You might think that the smaller something is then the easier it would be. In fact, the reverse is true. Not only does the soprano require a fair amount of physical intensity, it's also notoriously difficult to keep in tune. Everywhere I looked the advice was the same – this is not a beginner's instrument. And Raymond was fully on board with the orthodoxy.

But he did have an old alto he was keen to hire – an ideal instrument for a beginner. Now whilst there were plenty of alto players I could admire and even love from the history of jazz – Charlie Parker, Cannonball Adderley, Art Pepper, Johnny Hodges – these had never been my true heroes.

The top guys for me were always the tenor players like Coltrane, Sonny Rollins, Pharoah Saunders, Wayne Shorter, Lester Young, Stan Getz. And the tenor would probably have been my choice if I hadn't been a lifelong traveller. The size of a soprano would make it a lot easier for our imminent world tour – clearly not much had change since my choice of trumpet over trombone at the age of 11. Plus most tenor players also play the soprano – which makes sense as they are in the same key.

One of the things you have to get your head around when you start playing the saxophone is that it is a transposing instrument. This a technical term for the fact that when he invented it back in the 1840s, Adolphe Sax must have decided it would be a laugh if the note you played on the instrument wasn't actually the note you heard. In the case of a soprano and tenor, if you play a C what you actually get is Bb. With an alto or baritone, it comes out as Eb.

The whole idea clearly seems to have been designed to befuddle the poor brains of anyone who ever decides to start playing such a crazy instrument. In fact, it was even more of a jungle back in Sax's day because he also came up with versions pitched in C and F. And thereby comes the theoretical justification for this whole brain-twister. The idea was that depending on the pitch required you could play the same tune with exactly the same fingering but using a different instrument.

It's a bit like the blues harmonica – a very simple instrument that's available in a wide range of keys. So depending on the key of the tune you want to play, you whip out a fresh harmonica. But a saxophone is a fair bit bigger and most of us don't travel around with an unlimited supply of tunings. Which means you constantly have to transpose in your head if you're playing alongside a regular C instrument such as piano or guitar. Thanks a bunch Mr Sax.

By the way, can you believe the sax was actually invented by Mr Sax? Good job his name wasn't Higginbottom.

Anyhow, the point is that a soprano and a tenor are both tuned to Bb whereas an alto or baritone are tuned to Eb. Did I really want to start off with my head in the wrong department of this transposition nightmare when I already knew my ultimate destination? I argued my case for the soprano and Raymond said he would check if any of his students had an old one they wanted to sell. But in the meantime why didn't I hire the alto for six weeks?

There was of course also the disadvantage that I wouldn't immediately have that cool Coltrane look with the straight soprano I had been dreaming of. And I knew just how important the look could be from adolescent guitar posing. I'd even been checking out the best hat to complete the effect. That much was clear from all the gigs I'd been to – you can't play jazz if you ain't got a hat!

The alto seemed somehow to lack that innate sense of cool. But for six weeks I was prepared to give it a shot. So I took it home and proceeded to spend weeks specialising in out-of-tune farty noises. It's the stage in musical development that your nearest and dearest – and those not quite so near and dear – must dread. All we can do is smile and assure them it won't be long before they start to recognise a tune.

Unfortunately for our German lodger Alexander, the very first piece Raymond set for me to play was a tune he had spent a lifetime trying to forget. It meant absolutely nothing to me – I didn't even recognise it. But even in my first week on a new instrument kind of way, Alexander immediately heard the strains of an old German hymn that had been forced on him in primary school. My squeaky rendition was bringing back some painful memories.

Luckily for him I didn't dwell on it too long. Indeed Raymond didn't seem to think I was capable of dwelling on any kind of tune and became increasingly exasperated by my singular inability to keep time. I started to feel the shadow of school days hovering over me in a series of Miss Grant moments as I continued getting my semi-quavers and crochets in a twist.

I already recognised the impatience that had stopped me progressing on the guitar in my younger days. Maybe playing music simply wasn't for me. My desire to run before I could walk was born from an inbuilt sense that music was fun rather than work. And wasn't that the whole point – to have fun? But I had a foreboding that this idea of fun was entirely a result of my experience of music as a listener rather than a performer. Perhaps I wasn't cut out for all the hard work and discipline required to actually master an instrument.

At the same time I was already starting to hate that alto, blaming it for every wrong note. So I decided to go in search of the real thing – a soprano.

As it happened my luck was in. Brighton turned out to be one of the best possible places to find a quality used instrument.

At that time it was home to one of the best saxophone repairers and dealers in the country. Rupert wasn't just Mr Sax – he was Dr Sax.

Not realising visits were by appointment only, I tracked him down to the unmarked door of a shambolic mews garage. It didn't seem terribly promising. But once you'd stepped inside and become accustomed to the gloom, there was a veritable Aladdin's Cave to be unearthed. In the main workshop was the saxophone hospital with dozens of instruments in various stages of being stripped down. Along one wall and scattered around the rest of the room were hundreds of instruments of every age, size, colour and quality for sale.

It took some time to get up the courage to tell Rupert that a pathetic beginner like me was actually thinking of buying a soprano sax. In the meantime I listened to a fascinating monologue about all the jazz stars who regularly popped by and how I shouldn't ever buy a new saxophone because the old ones he sold and restored were so much better.

As time went on I finally got round to the point of my visit. He asked my budget. Of course the amount I had in mind didn't even approach the bottom of the range and the first one I pointed at was going for thirty times my maximum. Gulp. But he quickly understood where I was coming from and scooped up a few sopranos from the bargain shelf and suggested I try them out. Now this was going to be a challenge.

Seriously. How can I even think about playing in front of a sax doctor whose clients include the likes of Courtney Pine and Gilad Atzmon? Could I get away with the German Hymn if I jazzed it up a bit? Or maybe I could try my one and only scale? How about freeform farting? I might be able to pass it off as experimental avant-garde...

Somehow I managed to gather enough confidence to withdraw into the cupboard that passed for a practice room. The thrill of Dace's listening booth came flooding back – excerpt the smell of vinyl and stale tobacco had been replaced by brass polish.

I tried each instrument in turn and found them all a lot easier to play than Raymond's alto. Clearly I wasn't getting much of a tune but I was getting a sense of tone and playablility. As time went on there was one I kept coming back to.

"How are you getting on in there?"

"Fine thanks. I'm thinking this one might be OK."

He smiled.

"That's Ian Price's old soprano. Did you ever hear Ian play?"

Did I ever hear Ian Price? I loved Ian Price.

He had been a Brighton institution. Well, as much of an institution as you can be within the tiny jazz subculture of any town. But I'd seen him perform in local pubs on many occasions – mostly playing tenor but occasionally on soprano. I vividly recalled talking to him at a deserted Dorset Arms one evening after he had played Sonny Rollins' St Thomas. He played it so well and I told him it was one of my favourite tunes. He was a brilliant player. Sadly he had died at a tragically young age just six months earlier.

"His family asked me to sell his old instruments."

His eyes misted over.

"He was a beautiful person."

I looked down at the soprano in my hands and recognised this was destiny.

"He played it for years. He did get an upgrade when he came into some money a little while back. But that was his first soprano. Are you interested?"

I nodded enthusiastically. I didn't have to think about it. Here was an opportunity to buy a nice instrument at a good price. But I also felt an immediate affinity with Ian and a sense that if I could absorb just a fraction of his musical spirit then it would take me a long way as a talisman on the road ahead. My only worry was that I was unworthy of such a wonderful treasure.

As soon as I got home I took it out and started to play. Even though I clearly didn't have a clue what I was doing, I enjoyed every minute. The same couldn't be said for the dreaded alto I forced myself to practice in Eb ready for the week's lesson. The soprano was as much a liberation as the alto was a straightjacket. Nevertheless, I persevered for a few more weeks as I'd paid upfront and Raymond felt it was a better instrument on which to make my first baby steps.

I dutifully prepared by diligently slogging through my homework – but to no avail. It still sounded awful. That week's lesson was even more miserable than the last. I was clearly a huge disappointment as Raymond continued to shake his head at my inability to keep time or even hit a note. I was going nowhere fast.

Maybe my attention span just wasn't long enough but in the coming days my thoughts kept wandering back to the magic of the Ian Price soprano. The more I worked with the alto at exercises from Book One with the odd German Hymn thrown in for light relief, the worse it seemed to get. And the more I wanted to just let rip on the soprano.

The following week I decided to take it with me and proudly showed off my treasure. Raymond gave a quick sniff of disapproval and declared it to be hopelessly out of tune. I was crestfallen.

"Now let's get back to those exercises on the alto. One-and-two-and-three-and-four..."

I couldn't wait to get out of the room. The ghost of Miss Grant continued to loom as I quivered with fear. I started to realise I possibly had a pathological aversion to music teachers

Rupert had told me he'd give me a full refund if for any reason I didn't get on with the instrument. I made my decision. It clearly wasn't up to scratch and more importantly I was turning out to be a complete failure. It was time to take him up on the offer. I had tried and failed. I simply wasn't cut out to be a jazz musician.

But in the meantime, out of curiosity I bought an electronic tuner to check just how bad the tuning had been. To my surprise, after jiggling the mouthpiece a little, I found it was in fact pretty accurate. I turned my attention to the alto. No matter what I did, I couldn't make it so that one end of a scale was ever in tune with the other. I was beginning to get an idea as to why the soprano might sound so much better to my ears than the alto.

It was time for the final lesson of my package and I thought I'd done pretty well preparing for it in the circumstances. Raymond didn't agree. I hesitantly suggesting the possibly there might be a problem with the alto. He was shocked at the suggestion and told me the only way forward was more of the same. I should hire the alto for another six weeks and book another package of lessons. Perhaps given enough time, I might eventually start to show some improvement.

It's some measure of my music-teacher phobia that in my fear of upsetting him I was on the brink of accepting and paying up for another round of German Hymns. But thankfully at the last moment I gathered all my strength, left the dreaded alto behind and walked out the door. The sense of freedom was uplifting. My career as a saxophone player was over.

***

I had clearly been on the wrong track. But the failure of my musical education before it had even begun left a vacuum in my life. I was convinced the only way forward was to admit the whole idea had been a massive mistake. It was time to reclaim my normal life without the daily grind of scale practice. I would just explain to Angela that she had massively overestimated my capabilities, take the soprano back to Rupert and continue with our travel plans without all the added complications of squeezing a soprano sax into the luggage. Maybe I could go back to sketching or writing poetry instead. Something easy.

I dialled Rupert's number and prepared for all the ridicule I deserved for imagining I could go overnight from zero to hero just because I had bought an instrument that once belonged to a genius. But then right at the last moment I asked myself if there might be another option. I was just about to ask to return the saxophone when I hesitated and started down a completely different road. Isn't it remarkable the way big things in life can so often turn on a split second?

"Hi Rupert. It's Bob. I bought the Ian Price soprano from you."

"Oh, hi. How you getting on with it?"

"Fine. Well, that is, umm... The instrument is fine. But I'm not sure I'm doing so well."

"Oh?"

"Maybe it's just me but I didn't get very far with my teacher. Look I just had a thought. I was wondering if you might be able to suggest someone else?"

"A teacher?"

"I know it's not really your field but you must know a lot of sax players."

"Yeah, sure."

He didn't sound at all sure. But I ploughed on regardless.

"Except my last teacher was a bit too much of a teacher, if you know what I mean. And that doesn't really work for me."

"Errr. So you're looking for a teacher who's not a teacher?"

"Exactly! You've got it!"

Silence. Poor Rupert didn't have a clue what I was going on about. I had to think this one through quickly and work out what I was really looking for. Or else my only opportunity for salvation would be lost.

"It was all too much like being back at school. But I'm never going to be a musician – it's never going to be a profession for me. So I don't really want to go to school. What I want is to have fun. I'm looking for a teacher who can show me how to enjoy what I'm doing. Can you think of anyone?"

To his credit, Rupert didn't just tell me to stop bothering him with all this nonsense – which he had every right to do. He thought for another moment before finally replying.

"Leave it with me. I'll get back to you with a name."

And sure enough, a few days later the name arrived in a text message. And the name was – Björn.

***

We arranged to meet shortly afterwards at one of the cool but crumbling studios in the old arches under the railway station that he used for teaching and rehearsals. The place itself oozed the essence of jazz. It was an undeveloped island in what was starting to become a more gentrified quarter of town. You could have taken a grainy black and white photo of the exterior, added a puff of steam and you'd have the classic jazz album cover.

There were several rooms inside used for various musical activities. I managed to find someone and asked if they knew if Björn was around. They assured me that if he'd told me he was coming then he would surely be there – eventually. The time for our first lesson came and went with no sign from him. This was clearly going to be a very different experience from the precise military operation I'd been used to with Raymond.

After another 10 minutes or so he ambled in looking a bit lost, wearing ill-fitting clothes with a stubbly beard and greasy hair. But he had eyes that sparkled – and he was wearing a cool black leather hat. A jazz hat!

He looked the part and he was the part. He'd studied soprano and tenor saxophone (no alto!) for four years at the Royal College of Music in Stockholm and also played a wide range of other instruments – piano, accordion, clarinet, flute, ukulele, etc. He'd also travelled a lot with his music – performing with all kinds of great bands.

While he was at home, tiny jazz gigs in local bars were his passion. But he also had a regular meal ticket. Every summer he would tour stadiums, festivals and concert halls around the world starring as Benny Anderson in ABBA The Show – one of the leading ABBA tribute acts. Perhaps the hat was no accident. Despite first impressions, Björn was indeed a true performer.

Not that he told me any of this straight off. That was all for me to find out over time. It even took a few weeks until he'd admit he had a show right then in the fringe of the local arts Festival with his wife Maria called My Friend Lester – a musical exploration of the relationship between singer Billie Holiday and tenor sax player Lester Young.

But for that first lesson he was just a badly-dressed unpunctual shambles with a sax. He looked at me and smiled.

"So what do you want to do?"

"I want to have fun."

He nodded sympathetically as though he knew exactly what I meant.

"I had a few lessons. But, you know, I'm never going be a great musician or anything. But I love the soprano. I'd just like to be able to enjoy playing it."

"OK."

He picked up his sax.

"Can you play this?"

He played a single note. I looked at him and picked out the same note.

"What about this one?"

He played another note and I followed him.

"And this?"

We made our way from High C to Low C with just four notes in between then slipped up the scale a couple of steps before repeating the whole thing a few times.

"Now you just keep playing that same riff and I'll play some chords on the piano."

I couldn't believe it. This was sounding pretty good.

"That's brilliant. What is it?"

"It's a tune called Sonnymoon For Two by Sonny Rollins."

"You're kidding me? You mean I played a Sonny Rollins number? Without even knowing it? Wow!"

He smiled again. I was on board.

"Cool. Now you could try making a solo out of some those notes if you like."

What he didn't tell me was that the notes of the tune were simply a run down the notes of a minor pentatonic scale – the foundation of the blues and lots of jazz improvisation. But then he never did tell me anything about musical theory. He didn't need to. He just asked me to follow what he played and have fun. Perfect.

The following week we transposed the notes we had used for Sonnymoon and we had a whole new blues key at our disposal. Then in week three we were flying with Thelonious Monk through the jagged lines of Blue Monk. I was loving every moment and couldn't bear to put the instrument down. The transformation from Raymond's joyless basement couldn't have been greater.

I was forced to take a couple of weeks off when I had to go away for work but made up for lost time on my return with two lessons in two days. We started working on some scales – even that seemed like fun now – as well as stocking up on some new tunes – Summertime, Stella By Starlight, Stormy Weather.

I also put in a special request. One of my favourite movies of all time is The Wizard Of Oz – it seems to me to have such a universal mythology – and it also seemed to me that the soprano sax was an ideal instrument to play Somewhere Over The Rainbow. Björn's response was to scribble out a universal version using numbers rather than notes with a suggestion that I go away and try playing it in a variety of keys – but maybe to start out with F.

It was a great way into the tune and a great learning exercise. I really appreciated his willingness to free me from the tyranny of following dots on manuscript paper. He recognised where I was coming from and did his utmost to encourage my musical development in as a free a way as possible.

And it was working. I went Over The Rainbow crazy, spending the whole day working on it, milking every last drop. I'm sure some people may not share my enthusiasm. But it's a tune I still love and at that point it certainly helped me to love my saxophone.

I couldn't believe what was happening. I was still only a couple of months into my life as a soprano sax player and here I was already playing the kind of stuff I adored. I was only too well aware that this was the old run before you can walk routine all over again. But I didn't care. I could never see the point in wasting time on the boring stuff if you could go straight for the thrill. And with my 60$^{th}$ only days away I had no time to waste. I was ready for musical lift-off!

\*\*\*

The Björn experience had filled me with so much confidence that for a crazy moment I had considered accelerating the whole process and scheduling a live music element for my party. In the end I thought better of it. Best not get too carried away – especially when there was some serious celebrating to do. I was still a long way off performing when anything but stone cold sober.

However, the following day was different. This was my day for family. And it turned out to be a special one – a coming together. It also turned out to be one of the last major events before my sister Jenny became ill and passed away. We didn't know then we would be losing her so soon. But our mother had died a few years earlier and the family house had been sold. When clearing it we had found a bottle of Bordeaux that my grandmother had bought in the 1930s. The bottle had passed into family folklore as no suitable occasion had arisen over 80 odd years to drink it. We suspected it might be well be past its best. But that day we took the plunge, pouring a glass for each of six siblings.

We toasted each other and went on to drink what turned out to be the most delicious glass any of us had ever tasted. It was a moment I'm sure none of us will ever forget as we joined together over the family wine. In retrospect it was also a memorable moment of health to share with Jenny.

Neither will I ever forget what happened next. In response to a request from my sister in law Gillian, I unveiled my soprano. Fortified by ancient Bordeaux and the spirit of Ian Price and emboldened by laid-back Björn, I began to play Over The Rainbow.

I couldn't believe my own nerve at actually playing in public and was convinced I wouldn't make it through to the end. But I didn't stumble once. I got through the tune, let out a deep breath and looked around. My brother James – a man of few words – was first to speak.

"I'm impressed."

What a moment that was. Did it count as my first gig? Probably not. But my secret was out. I was learning the soprano sax. And I could already string a few notes together. The journey had begun.

# CHAPTER SIX

## Escape To Sicily
## – A New Life in the Mediterranean

The party had been the first weekend of May, leaving us a couple of days to prepare for the first of three blocks of three months away. The Sicilian adventure began all too promptly with an early alarm call on the day of my 60$^{th}$ birthday. The flight to Palermo took off at 05.55am on the fifth day of the fifth month to begin our three trips of three months. I'm sure Mr Chang would have approved the elegant numerical symmetry.

Things didn't immediately get off to such an auspicious start after landing though, with delays to all trains out of Palermo because of a demonstration on the tracks along the line at

Termine Imerese. But as the delay went on it became clear that this was in fact the perfect welcome to our new life. Frustration gave way to a sense of slowing down and getting into tune with a more relaxed rhythm. It was a way of life that followed the cycles of the day and the seasons – but also one that regarded blocking trains as fair game!

Angela took the time to continue reading a book on Sicilian lemons, which turned out to be a surprisingly diverse and interesting subject. Every so often she would look up and tell me another fascinating fact in the history of citrus cultivation. But above all, her respect was reserved for the cedro.

"Wow. We really have to find one of these while we're here. They're huge lemons with a really thick skin that you can eat. They sound amazing!"

Shortly after, our train was finally announced and we began the beautiful 80-kilometre ride east, along the north coast to Cefalù. I adore train journeys – even short ones. And this was a beautiful route, hugging the coast with a first sight of the gorgeous shimmering translucent blues of the Tyrrhenian Sea dancing like an impressionist painting. It was a suitable welcome.

We hopped off the train in Cefalù with our pile of luggage – topped off by a soprano saxophone in its new padded travelling case. We were immediately picked out and greeted by Rosario, the retired chemistry teacher from whom we had rented an apartment for the duration of our stay. He quickly ushered us outside to a beaten up old Fiat, barely big enough for us to squeeze into, surrounded by what felt like far too much stuff.

Just as well, it turned out to be only a few hundred metres later that we pulled up in the main thoroughfare of Via Roma and tumbled out. A gate led into the gorgeous garden behind our new flat, where we were greeted by a wonderful aroma. Angela looked around.

"What's that gorgeous smell? Is it honeysuckle?"

"No," replied Rosario. "It's the cedro tree – look."

He pointed to a tree in the corner with huge knobbly lemons the size of small melons hanging from it. In the kitchen, two more were in a bowl, ready for us to eat. I couldn't wait a moment longer – after all it was my birthday – cutting through one of them and offering a slice each to Angela and Rosario. They were utterly delicious. They tasted of Sicily.

***

One of the most important words in the Italian language is passeggiata – an evening stroll that is such an essential ritual of national life. For our first evening, we took our passeggiata along the shops of Via Roma as far as Piazza Garibaldi, at the start of the old town and a splendid spot for an aperitivo. We sat outside the Cafe Antica Porta Terra in the golden evening sun, sipping a Campari soda. The yellow stone of the facades of the buildings along Corso Ruggero were bathed in the same magical light. We just sat and drank it all in with huge smiles splashed across our faces. We had arrived.

With Angela being a UK-based Italian and me an incurable traveller, Italy had been a magnet ever since we had met. Within our first couple of months together we were already on our way down to Naples and the island of Procida, stopping off in Rome on the way back north to Lombardy, where Angela visited her family and I had a working trip to a film festival in Varese. It was a long way round – but the long way is always the best way to go.

Although other parts of the world were constantly calling, we always found time to return to Italy and within 18 months we managed our first whistle-stop visit to Sicily. Our most powerful memory of that trip was our arrival in Lipari – the largest of the Aeolian Islands and at that time still relatively unscathed by mass tourism. Our arrival back then had been uncannily similar to that first afternoon in Cefalù.

Stepping down from the ferry we had come across Stefano, who asked if by any chance we were looking for a place to stay. And of course we were. So he led us to a nearby apartment overlooking the sea – with a bowl of fresh lemons sitting in the window. That's all I needed in order to know I wanted to stay. There's a pattern here. I'm clearly a sucker for fresh lemons – or cedri. By the time we took the ferry to leave, we were already talking about coming back one day to live.

After a little time back in Brighton, Angela's desire to find a place in Italy continued to blossom. The only two things she was sure of were that it would not be in her home region of Lombardy and that, after half a lifetime in England, sunshine was an essential ingredient.

We spent time exploring Liguria with the idea of setting up a bed and breakfast there. The adventure even took us so far as putting in a speculative offer on a tiny old vineyard on the edge of the beautiful village of Dolceacqua – a crazy venture with no access, no level ground and no possibility of building more than a shed on the land. Luckily the project went no further.

But at the back of our minds there was always the idea of finding a home in Italy. Whenever we visited, we had half an eye on the potential of a local area. Finally our attention swivelled back to Sicily and I recalled that before that first visit, a friend had told me how much he had enjoyed Cefalù. Time hadn't allowed us to stop back then. But we did take the train along the coast from Palermo to Milazzo for the ferry to Lipari and I had caught a glimpse of Cefalù cathedral as we passed by.

The image stayed with us and we finally decided that it could potentially be what we had been searching for. So nine months before my birthday we had flown out for a week to check it out. Sure enough it ticked all the boxes – sunshine, sea, great beach, beautiful old town, incredible history, great location, less than an hour from Palermo and the National Park of the Madonie mountains rising up behind the town. The first part of the Year of Sixty had been decided.

And now we strolled along Corso Ruggero – the heart of the old town named after the Norman King who had enjoyed his time here so much that he had built a cathedral. He started work on the magnificent structure in 1151 and it was still unfinished when he died in 1154 – his wish to be buried there ignored as he was laid to rest in Palermo. It was finally consecrated in 1267 and remains a fitting and dominating memorial to this giant of Sicilian history.

Just as I had spotted it from the train several years earlier, the cathedral is impossible to miss – nestling beneath the huge and distinctive headland of La Rocca but towering in its turn above the maze of alleyways that make up the old town, sloping down towards the tiny old harbour.

We paused to look inside at the simple but magnificent interior, dominated by the huge mosaic of Christ Pantocrator – very similar to but predating the more celebrated one in Monreale Cathedral just outside Palermo. Together with Palermo's Cappella Palatina (Royal Chapel), the interiors of these two cathedrals are among the greatest treasures of the Arabo-Norman period. But there was one further local treasure that required our full attention as we passed by – the pastries glistening like so many precious jewels in the window of the pasticceria on the corner of the Piazza Duomo.

We continued on our way to check out the row of seafood restaurants backing onto the rocks below, in search of the ultimate birthday dinner. And we found the perfect table – perched all on its own at the end of a walkway above the waves. It was the ultimate romantic table for two, suspended above the crystal waters lapping the rocks below. Even from up there you could clearly see the fish and sea urchins beneath, through shifting shades of blue and purple as the sun began to settle on what had been a long but glorious day.

The colours of the sea will be my abiding memory of Cefalù, especially around sunset as they merge between bright blue, deep blue, cobalt and turquoise, mixed with multiple shades of green and a wonderful steel grey. There are the colours directly from the sea and then there is also the fading sunlight that plays on the sand, rocks and vegetation beneath. Smoky wisps of purple, violet and blue rise up in the mountains beyond the bay, surrounded by the oranges and reds of rooftops and the ochre and yellows of the buildings themselves These are the colours of Cefalù.

And then of course the food is such an utterly essential ingredient of life in Sicily – the freshest possible food with the most powerful tastes and aromas imaginable. It's food as I'm tempted to believe must have been everywhere in the world before it became just another commodity.

We breathed in the salty air as we took a good sniff and slurp of the local white wine made from the typically Sicilian Grillo grape. I already knew what I was going to order – the classic Palermitano dish pasta con le sarde. Sardine pasta may not sound like a classic. But the ingredients make this a signature dish for an island that throughout its history has been a cultural melting pot right at the heart of the Mediterranean, combining elements from both its African and European traditions.

First, you gently fry some chopped onion and drop in a few fresh anchovies, allowing them to melt into the pan. Throw in a handful of sultanas, some pine kernels plus a little saffron if you wish and splash the whole lot with white wine. The next ingredient is pure Sicilian sunshine – strattù. This is the most intense and wonderful tomato paste imaginable, made by spreading a mixture of fresh cooked tomatoes across a wooden surface and leaving it in the sun to dry. Then throw in some fresh fileted sardines and allow to simmer.

In the meantime prepare the pasta. Typically this would be buccatini – a substantial long pasta like very thick spaghetti with a small hole through the centre. The secret ingredient is to throw a bunch of finocchietto into the water together with the pasta. This is an essential flavour of Sicily – the leaves of the wild fennel that grows all over the island. As the sauce begins to thicken and stick, you should use some of the fennel flavoured water from the pasta pan to loosen and flavour it. Once the pasta and sauce are ready, combine the two and sprinkle with pangrattato – toasted breadcrumbs.

This is an absolutely typical finishing touch for many a Sicilian meal.

For me, the whole dish combines just about every element that makes Sicily so perfect. There was no other possibility for a first birthday meal. We ordered some simple fried calamari to follow – although in truth the pasta would have been quite enough.

Dessert? No competition. We lingered over the meal and wine and took in the sunset as day turned to night, unveiling an inky sky filled with what seemed like all the dazzling stars of the Ancient World. Then we made our way back to the Piazza Duomo. What else could we ask for to round off the evening but a classic Sicilian gelato from the local pasticceria?

***

Rosario and Salva were both retired teachers and proved to be the most welcoming landlords we could have hoped for. Like most middle-class Sicilians they were relatively affluent with government pensions and a property portfolio passed down through their families. Property is not something to trade in Sicily – it's to keep and improve for the next generation.

Although officially retired, Rosario never stopped working on one project or another. In between times he would find a moment to gather wild herbs and salads on his way home through the countryside – delivering them to us as a little gift. Like so many of his contemporaries, he lived to work and certainly didn't spend on luxuries. That beaten up old Fiat was his only means of transport apart from a little scooter he used to hop around town.

Our apartment was perfect, with its shady little garden filled with a colourful array of flowers. The interior was typically cool with its thick walls, high ceilings, ceramic floors and substantial shutters. Air conditioning had been added for the benefit of tourists but most locals would have been happy to depend on the natural cooling of the traditional building techniques.

One unintended benefit of the typical Sicilian interior was its incredible acoustic properties. I took my saxophone out of its case for the first time, selected a reed, fitted it to the mouthpiece and began to play. But I had to stop dead in my tracks to check it was really me. I started again and Angela popped her head around the door.

"Wow! That sounded amazing. You're really improving."

The sound was different from anything I had managed to produce back in Brighton. The acoustics of the room were so incredibly bright, kicking out a whole new tone with masses of reverb and echo. It made me feel I could actually manage to play this instrument after all.

I jumped into Over The Rainbow with renewed enthusiasm with solos and scales thrown in for good measure. And then I felt ready to move on with the rest of the new repertoire – Stormy Weather, Summertime, Stella By Starlight.

I also took the opportunity to start thinking about the sound I was producing by working on variations of my embouchure. Neither Raymond nor Björn had given much advice on the technical side of blowing so I took the opportunity to start working through this and was delighted to finally hit a high F.

The only problem was that I was convinced the additional volume of the natural acoustics of the apartment would eventually prove too much for our neighbours – and that meant our so-far kind and patient landlords.

I was absolutely right to believe I might be heard but quite wrong to believe I might annoy anyone. It wasn't long before I started to get appreciative nods and it became clear that Rosario and Salva were actually enjoying the process of working out the titles of the latest tunes I was tackling. After a while I decided to work on something just for them so I made a stab at O Sole Mio.

The next time I saw them they were extremely kind about my playing. I had an Italian audience!

\*\*\*

Now it was all very well to be playing. But if I really wanted to get anywhere on the sax the time had clearly come for that jazz hat. Of course a hat doesn't do anything to help you play. But so many jazz musicians seem to wear a hat on stage – like the famous pork pie hat that became Lester Young's trademark. or Thelonious Monk and his short-brimmed trilby or Sinatra's Fedora.

It was becoming clear to me that none of them could have reached the musical heights without their respective hats. I'd vote for anything that cuts down on the sheer hard graft involved. If Sicilian acoustics could make me sound better and a Sicilian hat could make me look better then I was all for it!

Strictly speaking though it actually all had a lot more to do with climate than music. The sun was scorching hot every day and some kind of protection was becoming essential. But clearly I would need something with a Sicilian flavour. And so much the better if it could double as a trademark jazz accessory!

I'd already noticed Augustino's shop not far from the cathedral down in the old town. He specialised in the classic Sicilian coppola or flat cap. I strolled in trying to look super-cool.

"Buongiorno. Can I help you?"

"I'm looking for a coppola."

He smiled and waved his arm in a huge arc as if to say I was clearly in the right place. He sold nothing else – every square centimetre was covered with stacks of the things.

I rummaged around and tried a few on. But none of them would fit. Which is basically why I don't often wear a hat in the first place – my head is rather large and it's always difficult to find anything in my size. I looked up sheepishly.

"C'è qualcosa più grande?"

Augustino stretched out a hand for a box nestling under his desk – the supersize department.

"Certo. Magari uno di questi."

I peered inside and quickly worked out that these were indeed a bunch of fashion remnants suitable only for an oversized freak such as myself. However I persevered and right at the bottom, beneath the hideous and forgotten trends of yesteryear, was lurking what I thought might just be a passable jazz accessory. I tried it on and looked in the mirror.

"Perfect. Now all I need is to learn how to play."

"Scusi?"

I explained that I was learning to play the saxophone and that I was interested in any musical events that might be taking place locally. He told me that there would indeed be a concerto the following week at the town's theatre – a beautiful building that had been closed for quite some time and had only opened rarely since its restoration. As we continued to chat, I made a mental note to be there.

I left the shop proudly wearing my new coppola. Indeed it became a permanent fixture from that point on. So the following morning it was already firmly in place as we made our way to the railway station to catch a train into Palermo for a day of sightseeing.

We bought our tickets in the station bar and as we had plenty of time to spare ordered a coffee and cornetto – the croissants that in Sicily are stuffed to bursting point with a variety of delicious fillings. For me the best is the ricotta that finds its way into so much of the island's cuisine. But chocolate, pistachio, custard cream and jam are frequent alternatives.

As I was paying, the girl behind the counter looked at my hat and smiled.

"Mi piacce la tua coppola – I like your cap."

"Grazie."

"You bought it from my father."

"How do you know where I bought it?"

"Because I recognise the material. My father is Augustino."

Content that my hat was as distinctive as I had imagined it to be, we jumped on board the Palermo train. With no set plan, on our arrival we wandered through the streets of the Kalsa district. On Via Garibaldi we came across a hat shop. Actually it sold nothing but coppole. And there right in the middle of the window was my hat – or at least another hat in exactly the same style. Possibly it wasn't quite the one-off I had imagined.

We went inside. The proprietor looked at me and nodded.

"You have the same hat as I have in the window."

"Yes, I bought it in Cefalù."

"Ah, from Augustino?"

"Certo."

"He is my friend."

At that very moment the phone rang and he excused himself to answer it. But seconds later a big smile appeared on his face and he looked up.

"It's Augustino. He's placing an order."

We left the two of them to their business call, increasingly aware that in Sicily everyone is connected – even by hats.

We did a frantic round of the most unmissable sights – the Capella Palatina, the cathedral, Quattro Canti and the Pretoria Fountain, a tour of the Teatro Massimo opera house, the Martorana and the incredible Serpotta interiors of the Oratorios of Santa Cita, San Lorenzo and San Domenico. A tour of the street markets of Balarò, Capo and Vucceria proved to be just as impressive as any of the historical and architectural sights.

It was in the Vucceria that I had my first experience of yet another of my all-time favourite local dishes. Spaghetti ai ricci di mare is sea urchin pasta and the recipe is simplicity itself. Cook the pasta and stir in the delicate orange lobes of the sea urchin together with plenty of olive oil. Optional extras are some lightly fried garlic and chopped parsley. That's it. And it's absolutely delicious. It smells and tastes like the sea with a delicate hint of wild truffles.

The Vucceria is home to all manner of wonderful street food. Later every evening it turns into a huge outdoor bar. Palermo is one of my favourite places on Earth – far too intense to live there permanently we decided but hard to beat as a place to visit. And there's certainly no stopping you if you're wearing a genuine Augustino coppola!

# CHAPTER SEVEN

## O Sole Mio – Music and Gelato under the Italian Sun

Sunrise and sunset were sublime almost every day with colours pouring across the sky from a solar paint pot – a palette of purple, violet, crimson and gold making clear we were at the very heart of the Mediterranean. But in between came scorching sunshine, getting warmer by the day as the Sicilian cauldron began to simmer.

The heat is an essential element of Sicily's identity and for me it certainly proved one of its great pleasures. But there are plenty of occasions when it's time to cool off. A dip in the sea is one tempting solution. The other is to call on Sicily's greatest culinary contribution – ice cream.

Both gelato and ice-based granita go back in time to way before the advent of refrigeration. Indeed, the snow and ice of mount Etna and other high peaks were a valued commodity back in the Ancient World. Ice caves were used to keep it cool and it was even possible to export to neighbouring territories.

But the origins of our current treats are reckoned to date to the Arabic period over a thousand years ago and their sarbat – a combination of fruits and chilled water. This eventually became granita with the addition of crushed ice. Almond, pistachio and coffee are particularly popular these days as well as lemon and a range of fruits such as mulberry. Gelato came as a further development with the addition of milk and was the forerunner to ice cream all around the world. But I challenge you to find anywhere that offers quite such a delicious experience as that found in its Sicilian homeland.

We soon discovered that Sicilians have taken the art of ice cream consumption to a level way beyond anything the rest of us can dream of. I'm thinking of what I regard as the pinnacle of Sicilian cuisine – gelato con brioche. This is a dish for which I generally offer the rather prosaic translation of "ice cream in a bun". And that is precisely what it is.

Can you imagine a finer breakfast on a hot day than a fresh brioche sliced in two and crammed with the best ice cream you ever tasted – in any combination of flavours? To be honest, the only competition comes in the shape of its close cousin granita con brioche. In this case the two elements are served separately – your chosen flavour of iced granita served with fresh cream on top and brioche on the side to scoop the whole lot up. Heaven!

My pistachio granita stared up at me as I took a first glorious dab with my brioche. We were sitting at a table outside one of our favourite gelaterie just across the promenade from the sea, gazing along the shore towards the Porta Ossuna – the ancient western gateway into the old town – taking in the whole vista of Cefalù with its cathedral towers stretching up towards La Rocca, the town's history spread out before us. I took another thoughtful scoop with a morsel of brioche savouring its buttery hint of citrus.

We had barely been in Sicily a week but I knew something was missing. And Angela could tell.

"So what is it? You've been sitting there in silence right the way through your granita, staring into space as usual. You're time traveling again, aren't you?"

I smiled.

"Aren't you happy?"

"Of course I'm happy. Just look around. We're in Paradise. Look at all that history – we're in a world where the heritage is part of everyday life. We're so connected. And we're learning all about Sicily – its history, its people, its culture, its food. I've got my music, I've got granita – and I've Got You, Babe."

"But?"

"But if I'm going to fit in, I need to be able to do all that but in your language."

"That'll take time. And it's not as if you don't know any Italian."

"I need more. I need to go to school."

*** 

So there it was. I'd set myself yet another challenge and on Monday morning I was walking up the stairs of the local language school and nervously poking my head around the door.

"Buongiorno. Sono Bob."

I received a big welcome from Vittoria – perhaps not too surprising as the only other student who had been due that day hadn't turned up. This week it would be a class of one – which suited me just fine.

Tuition was a little briefer on a one-to-one basis, giving me more spare time for other activities. But more importantly it meant I could spend a whole week brushing up on the basics before anybody else arrived to see what a dunce they had been landed with.

Although we sketched out a basic learning scheme, we actually spent most of the morning chatting in simple Italian about my background and the crazy idea of learning the saxophone in a year on three continents. Vittoria had come across some pretty mad schemes in her time but this was a first even for her.

"There's going to be a concert at the theatre on Friday," she told me. "You might like to go as you're interested in music."

"Ah, yes. Someone already mentioned it to me."

"Who was that?"

"Augustino."

"Of course, the hat man."

"Certo."

The morning flew by and before I knew it our time was up. I was on my way home, calling Angela to meet for a coffee across the road at Giuseppe's.

Although there are many bars in Cefalù – just as there are in every Italian town – it's essential to realise from the outset that a bar is not just a place to drink coffee. Its social and political functions are far more important.

It's quite true that we did move around town sampling the competition – and I could write a whole book on the delights of the typical Sicilian bar. In the morning there's an incredible range of cornetti, ravioli and sfolie on offer. At lunchtime you might be tempted by an arancino – a fried stuffed rice ball – or possibly an impanate – a savoury pastry pie. Later in the afternoon you might be ready for a cannolo – a pastry shell crammed with sweetened ricotta. At any time of day the dolci di mandorla – little almond cakes – are a perfect accompaniment to your coffee.

Our three months in Sicily were about finding a new home. Food and culture were an essential element in that. But there was a bigger picture in getting to know the place and finding out if we were going to fit in. So on the day we arrived we realised we would have to identify a local bar to provide an anchor in the community. And that was Giuseppe, a mine of information. This is the function of all traditional bars in Italy – the main reason you go there is not for coffee but for the latest news.

In our case, however, Giuseppe had his work cut out. I think he felt rather sorry for these two outsiders who knew so little about the local gossip – one of whom struggled to understand much at all. So bit by bit he filled us in on the scandals, the politics, the personalities, the local events and an entire history of the town.

"And by the way," he added. "There's going to be a concert at the old theatre on Friday..."

***

My time was filling up fast but music remained a key part of the day. I had recognised however that there was no point in trying to do too much too soon – I simply wasn't ready. Before leaving for Sicily I had had six lessons with Raymond and five with Björn – a total of 11 sessions. There would be no more personal instruction while I was here so my task, so far as I could make out, was simply to become more familiar with the instrument.

I had brought a selection of music along with me. Simply interpreting the dots was a challenge in itself because I had never learned to sight-read. But so long as I knew the tune, I could pick my way through and eventually play a reasonably fluent rendition. This wasn't something that necessarily required a teacher. It just meant spending enough time playing a tune over and over until my fingers got the hang of where they were supposed to go.

The concept of muscle memory is a wonderful thing in music. My brain is stuffed with so much nonsense that if I had to remember the notes of every tune I wanted to learn then I'd never get past the first chorus. But by repeatedly playing an instrument, your fingers end up knowing where they need to go – as if by magic. And magic was something I needed if I was ever going to crack this insane challenge.

I suppose it's basically a matter of passing the memory of a tune down into your subconscious by playing it often enough so that your body can take over. But in order for that to happen, your fingers need to have become utterly familiar with your instrument – as if it is an extension of your body. And that was the process now facing me. I knew there wasn't much else I could learn from a teacher until I had established that level of familiarity.

So my task every day was simply to play. And it seemed to me that overdoing things could be just as bad as not doing enough. So I restricted myself to an hour of intense practice – generally in the morning when I was feeling relatively fresh. This is a habit that I have maintained ever since. Although the amount of playing time might vary, I have found that working on new material in the morning is much more beneficial. Once I became more proficient I found evenings could be good to let rip – but that's another part of the story.

Sharing time with other projects and the rest of our blossoming life in Sicily was all part of the process. I wanted to learn the saxophone but I wanted to learn it mindfully.

There were distinct elements facing us in each of our three-month journeys during the course of the year. The first was to experience a new beginning and see if we could find a sense of home here in Sicily. The second in the USA would be for Angela to further her training in yoga and meditation and for me to explore and hopefully take the music further – perhaps not such different objectives when it came down to it. The third in Asia would hopefully take us both deeper into an exploration of the mindful spiritual whole. One thing was already clear though. Whatever we went through during the course of the year, it couldn't and shouldn't be rushed.

Our daily schedule was certainly filling up. Angela had a little more slack than I did – which she used to good effect, socialising with neighbours, chatting to Giuseppe and the other traders and gathering local contacts and information, while also working on her yoga and meditation practice.

My own typical day started early, with a morning jog along the beach in the golden sunrise – stopping off at the bakery on my way back to pick up breakfast. After my shower I would head into school for two or three hours, depending on the number of students that day. After a quick coffee I would then fit in an hour or so of saxophone practice before lunch.

The afternoon would be more relaxed as the day continued to sizzle. We generally sat in the garden for a while where I would write my diary and perhaps sketch a few flowers (drawing was another new activity that I developed during our stay – the more new activities the better so far as my brain cells were concerned). I would then tackle my Italian homework and any musical preparation I might have unearthed during morning practice. At the end of the afternoon we would go for a stroll, possibly taking in a swim, possibly taking in a cannolo, very likely taking in an aperitivo.

As we passed Piazza Garibaldi I would look longingly at the row of old men who had congregated on benches, chatting for hours, simply happy to be there and pass the time of day.

"That's what I want to do," I used to tell Angela.

"Grow old?"

"Yes. And sit on a bench and chat to all the other old men."

"While your wife's at home cooking dinner, I suppose?"

It was a fair point. But it was also incredibly refreshing to see just how much time the old men of the town spent sitting and talking with each other. There's nothing unusual in this. You'll see the same thing in many town squares at the end of the day. And it was always this way in societies through the course of history. But we have lost our way in the modern world. A return to the simplicity of sitting on a bench as the sun went down was all part of the attraction of a move to Sicily so far as I was concerned.

It was already Thursday evening and there had been no further news of the concert that everyone seemed to know was happening tomorrow evening. So we decided to wander home past the Teatro Cicero. Sure enough someone had pasted a sheet of paper on the door: Concerto. Venerdì. 19.30.

It was brief, to the point, rather last minute and lacking any detail regarding the content of the performance. But seeing as how everyone in town already seemed to know about it, perhaps even that much wasn't strictly necessary.

My musical development in Cefalù had risen way above anything I might have imagined. However, we had been disappointed that there had been no opportunities to hear any live jazz while we were there. This was finally our chance for some live music – Friday night was booked.

***

The following evening we decided to arrive well before the curtain was due up in order to get a seat. But even though we were over half an hour ahead of time that was easier said than done. We should have realised that seats would be at a premium with no charge for admission, the theatre only occasionally being open and everyone in town being in on the secret.

The outside of the theatre revealed little of its splendour but once inside it was an absolute jewel, well worth the council's recent restoration. Originally built in 1814 it was a mini opera house in the classic style. The following year we went to a performance of La Traviata in Palermo's Teatro Massimo – one of the three largest opera houses in Europe – an unforgettable experience. But in its own intimate way, Cefalù's Teatro Cicero was just as special.

We pushed through the plush velvet curtains to see that all the stalls were taken. I scanned around three tiers of balcony boxes to see there was a little space up above and close to the stage. So we scampered up the stairs and claimed two of the last available places, peering around the auditorium to see all the familiar faces from our first few weeks in town. Augustino was there with his daughter, Giuseppe with his gorgeous Ukrainian wife, the lady from the bakery with a well-dressed young man and Rosario and Salva gave us a cheery wave from a box over on the far side.

We were all sat on beautiful red velvet chairs and the painting on the ceiling had been intricately restored. It was as though we were in a movie set. And in a way we were. This was one of several locations in Cefalù used by director Giuseppe Tornatore in his film Cinema Paradiso.

The secret of the mass turnout was revealed when the curtains finally swept open to reveal a huge banner: Chi chiude il Centro Nasceti, dice NON alla vita. It was only then that we realised the evening was a protest by the local council at the decision by the Regional Government to close the local maternity hospital. The whole event was far more of a test for my shaky Italian than a musical treat, with an endless stream of speeches from baby-hugging politicians before a final flurry of local talent was finally allowed on stage.

But at least we had been inside the theatre and we had been seen to be part of the local community. Indeed this seemed to be the essential element of the evening for most of those present. But as a musical event it was a disaster and I was starting to wonder if such a thing could even exist in Cefalù.

But the town's reputation was salvaged in a most unlikely way. Having finally reached the end of the "performance" and spoken with all our new friends, we made our way out of the theatre for a passaggiata through town. And up ahead we heard a glorious sound. But where was it coming from?

The only light we could see as we approached was from an old barber's shop tucked away in one corner. And sure enough, as we arrived outside we could see that the interior was crammed with musicians playing wonderful traditional music. We stayed to watch and soon enough a small crowd had gathered to enjoy the spontaneous concert. We stayed until the lights went out on what turned out to be an absolutely splendid gig.

\*\*\*

The next day I decided I needed my first Italian haircut. No prizes for guessing where I went.

Retracing my steps of the previous evening, I made my way directly to the bygone world of the old town hairdresser's. I popped my head around the door and walked straight into the distinguished-looking old man who had been singing and playing guitar the previous evening. A younger version of himself who had been playing mandolin was already cutting another customer's hair. Corrado smiled and indicated the empty chair in front of him.

"Accomadati."

So I made myself comfortable and enjoyed not only an excellent haircut but also Corrado's tales of the history of the shop – which had been in his family for generations and was now in the process of being handed on to his son. But it seemed to me that some of the implements hanging from the wall were a little too gruesome to be hairdressers' tongs.

"Ah, you noticed. We don't use those anymore. But there was a time when the barber in every small town doubled as the dentist. Those were my grandfather's tools."

There were also dozens of wonderful old black and white photographs of members of the family working in the shop. And it was clear that each generation had not only been barbers and dentists but also musicians.

"Yes, my father and my grandfather before him both played in a gruppo folklorico and my son now plays with me in the Cantatori di Dafne. You must come along this evening. It's the opening of the Regatta so there's a degustazione in Piazza Apollo and we'll be playing a little concert."

"I already saw you play. Last night – right here in the shop."

"Then you know what we will sing. You will have to join in! Can you remember the words in Siciliano?"

So our musical weekend was well and truly rescued. Once again we arrived early, this time to discover free seafood and white wine being distributed in the piazza by the mayor. Shortly afterwards Corrado and the Cantatori di Dafne took to the stage and played a dynamite set of Sicilian folk songs. We drank, danced and sang along as best we could. Music had finally arrived in Cefalù!

## BOB SWAIN

***

I continued with my programme of musical and linguistic education right through until the day that Sicily caught fire. We had been anticipating the event for a while with forecasts predicting a sudden increase in temperature and the arrival of incredibly high winds. And that could only mean one thing.

A Scirocco is a desert wind that blows from the south-east, picking up speed and heat as it travels across the Sahara. Sicily catches the initial blast furnace effect before the arrival of the blood-red rain that covers everything in Saharan sand. Everyone at the school that day was muttering darkly about the heat and as I walked back along the seafront I noticed that the lidos were all busy dousing their thatched roofs with water in preparation.

Sure enough, we woke the following day to incredibly high winds and outside it felt like an oven – a fan-assisted oven. Many years previously I had travelled in the Sahara and the feeling was all too similar.

The young lads running our favourite vegetable shop were from up in the hills near Cerda. They told us that it had been very difficult that morning as their smallholding had been surrounded by fire. Our neighbour Rosario popped by to say there had been fires not far away in Lascari and when we took a walk to the beach we could see the sky had an ominous glow. It was heavy and dark with dust and there was an ever-present smell of smoke in the air.

We didn't stay out long, opting to shut ourselves indoors for the day to avoid breathing in too much of the choking air. Checking the Internet I discovered that the railway and motorway had both been closed. We were cut off from the outside world.

We kept the windows firmly shut and the air conditioning switched on right through the day. There was nevertheless a strong smell of smoke and a constant sound of sirens outside.

The following morning it seemed cooler and the wind had dropped so I decided to go for my usual morning run along the beach. I couldn't believe it when less than a kilometre from our apartment I reached the burned out remains of Le Vele restaurant. The high ground above had been burnt as far as the road and railway line. The hillsides all around town were black and smouldering.

On the way home I looped past the football pitch run by the local church only to discover an emergency medical centre had been set up together with a whole fleet of ambulances. It finally dawned on me that there had been a full-scale emergency overnight and we had managed to sleep through the whole thing!

\*\*\*

After the fires, came the rain and the red dust of the Sahara left behind on the cars and windows. Then soon enough life was back to normal, late spring gave way to high summer and the full flood of tourists began to pile into town.

We had enormously enjoyed our time in in Cefalù and it had delivered everything we had asked of it. I had improved my Italian and made a good start on my saxophone playing. We had learned a lot about Sicily and the Sicilians and the island was becoming a place we could indeed call home.

But we had also come to realise that Cefalù was an intensely seasonal place. It was incredibly beautiful and had a rich cultural history. But at its heart it was a small provincial town that would contract to its core in the winter, only opening again as the visitors arrived. It simply didn't possess a cultural heart of its own – as we had noticed from the lack of major musical events. Perhaps it was simply too close to the bustle of Palermo.

So we reluctantly decided that while we were keen to settle in Sicily, perhaps Cefalù was a little too quiet for us. On the other had, Palermo was too hectic. We needed to find something in between.

We set off on a grand tour of the island, taking in the magnificent hill towns of the Madonie and the Nebrodi. We made our way through the interior up to Enna, beyond to the ceramics centre of Caltagirone and through the high country behind Palermo to Corleone. We headed west to Trapani, Marsala and Mazara del Vallo. We took in the temples of Segesta, Selinunte and Agrigento and the Roman Villa of Casale. We explored the slopes and vineyards of Mount Etna and nearby towns such as the pistachio capital of Brontë. We explored the tourist hotspots stretching along the east coast around Taormina and we returned once more to the volcanic cones of the Aeolian Islands scattered along the northern coast. Our return to Lipari was particularly educational. Tourism had taken off big time since our first visit. We also realised once again that off-season isolation was not for us. Like so much of Sicily, the islands offered a great deal as places to visit – but not a permanent home.

It was when we arrived in the south-eastern corner of Sicily that we finally came to feel a stronger attraction – in particular the ancient town of Siracusa and its historic heart of Ortigia. Dating back more than 2700 years, this was one of the earliest Greek settlements. Indeed in its day it was one of the grandest and most powerful cities of the Ancient World – and it still carries a sense of that greatness today.

Its sense of history is everywhere – perhaps nowhere more graphically than in the walls of its cathedral which started life as a Greek temple and went on to become a Byzantine church, a Mosque, a Norman cathedral and finally a Baroque cathedral. Its entire history is written right there in the walls with the original 2500-year-old Doric columns of the temple of Athena still embedded within them.

It was a large enough town that it had a life all of its own beyond the tourist season but had also attracted enough permanent settlers from other parts of the world to give it a lively cosmopolitan feel alongside its historic roots. In some ways it seemed to offer much of what we already loved about Brighton – except it was in Sicily. The more we wandered the twisting alleyways of Ortigia, the more we realised this was where our hearts belonged.

Time was up. But before leaving we found a place to rent for the following year. If all went well we would find our new home once we had completed the remaining two parts of the Year of Sax.

# CHAPTER EIGHT

## Intermezzo
## – Duets with Björn

Back in Brighton, we decided to try out a new pizzeria on our first night and discovered the manager was from Cerda – the same small town in the hills above Cefalù where the youngsters running the veg shop had their smallholding. And of course he knew them all – and their fathers and grandfathers. The connectedness of Sicilian life continued even once we were back in the UK.

That weekend, I was also able to catch up with live music by dipping into the Love Supreme jazz festival, which rolls into a nearby patch of the South Downs each summer. Hugh

Masekela and Terence Blanchard were among the year's jazz highlights. But the star of the show was Van Morrison.

Now Van is someone I've seen performing on countless occasions since I first caught him on stage back in 1974 and at his best I think he's one of the greatest jazz singers of all time. But over that time he has always been either utterly brilliant or utterly dire – so I was far from certain what to expect. Luckily, this time around he was inspired by the festival and played a storming set of largely jazz and blues material – featuring quite a bit of his own underrated but excellent saxophone playing.

It was enough to inspire me for the next few days – although Björn was away on tour so I wasn't able to fit in any lessons before I had to leave the country once again. I had been booked by the travel company I often worked with to check out the logistics for a new tour of the southern states of the USA. It was a full-on trip that would allow no opportunities for playing. So the soprano stayed in its case at home.

Nonetheless it was a chance to scout some of the musical locations where I would spend a lot more time later in the year. It was a first time for me in both Nashville and Memphis but a welcome return to the streets of New Orleans where the origins of jazz hung in the air.

My first visit had been 30 years earlier and my second 10 years after that. Just like this time, both occasions had been the height of summer and sweltering hot. Armstrong Park had supposedly been off-limits when I was first in town. But I went nonetheless and marched along with one of the earliest line-ups of the wonderful Rebirth Brass Band – still going strong today.

I had plenty of sweet memories of the bars and streets of the birthplace of jazz and knew I'd be adding to them soon enough. This trip was too busy to provide much in the way of musical opportunities. But I was already getting excited about the possibilities that lie ahead in part two of the Year of Sax.

\*\*\*

Back in Brighton, I jumped straight into a double lesson with Björn, who claimed to be impressed with the development of my playing in such a short time. He reckoned my breathing, embouchure and sound were all well on track. Predictably enough he said the biggest weakness was my timing – something that required hard work rather than just enthusiasm.

I was becoming aware of just how lazy I had been in Cefalù – even though it didn't seem that way at the time. It had been a lot easier to concentrate on sound than rhythm. But getting a handle on timing was essential if I was ever going to play successfully with other people. And I was getting the message loud and clear from Björn that it was time to start working.

As a first step, he provided me with recordings of himself so I could play along at home. Finally, I was playing Over The Rainbow with the correct note values. Only when I'd got the timing right did he allow me to look at the sheet music so I could see how it would be represented on paper.

When we met again we stuck with the same tune but started working with a recorded backing track. I was encouraged to play along with the chords by feel rather than by counting. It was a scary process but extremely useful. I've never been able to count my way through a tune but listening and intuitively following the line presented a way forward. Ultimately it's a matter of playing mindfully – being in the flow – focused on the moment.

In the same lesson we started picking apart the chords into their minor or major arpeggios – playing the first, third or fifth note of each. I didn't quite realise it at the time but Björn was helping me take my first baby steps into the world of jazz theory and improvisation.

Even though this was basement level stuff, it seemed pretty advanced at the time and I had no expectation of immediate results. But I could sense a door opening and managed to catch a glimpse of a wonderful world of music lurking on the other side. For the first time in my life I was getting an idea of what it must be like to actually play for real.

I even started to believe there was a possibility of reaching my goal within this lifetime. But there was so much ground to cover and I was 60 already!

***

I worked on it day by day at home and finally managed to play all the way through Over The Rainbow in time with a simple piano accompaniment. I felt like I'd made a major breakthrough. And I suppose that seeing as how I'd been playing for less than six months, it probably was.

We kept going with Over The Rainbow for the next lesson as I played with Björn's accompaniment and we continued breaking down the chords into their constituent notes. I was being fed the necessary tools to continue my journey.

"You know what?" he asked. "When we first start to play we can sometimes make some pretty cool sounds. But then we have to learn to play and there can be a long gap before we ever sound that good again."

"That seems right. I think I'm moving forwards though. It certainly feels like progress. But it's tough. And I don't sound nearly as good as I did a few weeks ago in Cefalù."

"You're going to sound much better. Just wait."

\*\*\*

The following day, my John Coltrane obsession continued with the acquisition of a new 4-CD set of recordings from live concerts in Europe from 1961. It's a stunning record of a musician who was exploring new corners of his music every single day. I soon realised it was recorded only two weeks after another box set I already had from New York concerts and yet his music had already progressed to another level. Coltrane was my God so I could hardly believe it when I arrived for my final lesson before leaving for the States.

"So what shall we play today?" asked Björn.

"You mean we don't have to do Over The Rainbow again?"

"We can do anything you like."

"Even Coltrane?"

"Of course. How about My Favourite Things?"

So we jumped straight in and I soon began to realise why Coltrane was so drawn to the piece. Even as a complete novice I could feel the attraction of those open spaces driven along by the minor key, seeming to resolve into sunlight as the brief major section arrived. I knew this was a tune I would play again and again over the coming years.

Not content with my joy at playing my favourite tune, Björn also started noodling on another pattern of notes and asked me to copy him as we played our way into the motif from Coltrane's A Love Supreme.

"This is it! This is why I started playing soprano sax in the first place!"

He nodded and smiled. We both knew that this was the material I needed to help me move to the next level – the material I would need to take with me on the second part of the Year of Sax.

# CHAPTER NINE

## American Odyssey
## – On The Road Again

We arrived in Portland, Oregon at the beginning of September – a wonderful laid-back hip city with brewery pubs on every corner and plenty of bargain shops for old books, classic vinyl and vintage clothing. Luckily this was our first stop so we knew we couldn't overstuff our bags so early in the trip. As it was I did pick up a great second-hand biography of Coltrane and a couple of his original albums. We missed out on Jimmy Mak's Jazz Club but still had a great few days before picking up a hire car on Angela's birthday and heading down the Columbia River Gorge to Mount Hood.

Having stopped off at the Timberline Lodge – used as the setting for Jack Nicholson's descent into madness in The Shining – we thought we had found ourselves caught up in the movie when 30 minutes later we pulled up outside our cabin to see someone walk by carrying a full-sized human skeleton! Despite the bizarre neighbours, we had an enjoyable and memorable stay out there in the woods.

As soon as we got inside I pulled out my sax and started to play, discovering that it had taken on the most glorious rich sound. Travelling with an instrument teaches you something about the importance of acoustics in music. The apartment in Sicily had been utterly magnificent with its forceful, loud tone and lots of reverb. This was quite different – warm, woody and cosy.

Entranced by the sound, I continued to play and it seemed to me I was doing pretty well. The American tour was underway and I had come to realise what a great idea it had been to travel with an instrument. The sax was taking on characteristics of each place we visited – seeming to reflect its environment. Was it just a matter of acoustics or was I starting to adapt as I travelled?

***

The next six weeks were to take us through Oregon, Colorado, New Mexico and California. Once Angela had booked into her ashram I would then have time to myself out in the California woods before flying across to Atlanta to lead a couple of tours through the Deep South.

As we drove down the glorious Oregon coastline, we stayed and I played in a succession of cabins – each one with its own individual character and tone. By the time we arrived in state capital Eugene, I had managed to forget all the crucial timing and rhythm exercises Björn had tried to hammer home. It was the same old story. I was having fun – like Sicily all over again but just a further on down the road.

We jumped on board a train in Eugene and rode all the way out to Grand Junction, Colorado, where we picked up another car and took a mazy run south through the glorious autumn trees of Colorado and into the red rock desert of New Mexico. Our first stop of any length was in tiny Albiquiu – where Angela's favourite artist Georgia O'Keefe had formerly based her studio and home.

It had been attracting artists ever since and was also home to Wanda – a wonderful elderly lady we'd met years before in East Africa. She was far tougher than travellers half her age and we had kept in touch. Her adobe house offered yet another wonderful sound and for a couple of days I would take my sax down to the bottom of her garden and onto the banks of the Chama River.

It was a truly inspiring setting and I had a real sense of the spirit O'Keefe had drawn upon for her work. I also realised it

THE JOY OF SAX

was not just tone but also some indefinable spirit that seemed to be entering my saxophone and affecting my playing as I travelled. I continued to justify my laziness by revelling in the experience of the sound I was making. Technique could wait a while longer until I was back in Brighton with Björn. This was too precious to miss.

***

Music gave way to art as we explored the pueblo of Taos and the galleries of Santa Fe – a wonderful cultural trail before taking a magnificent long drive back up to Mesa Verde and a blissful stay by the banks of the Marcos River with hosts Bryan and Sarah. Surrounded by beautiful trees, with stunning views of the mountains – including Mesa Verde itself – I made the most of every moment, playing down by the river, inspired by the natural bounty of such an incredible setting.

As I played, a group of wild turkeys scuttled by – adding yet further to the rural dreamscape. It was only later that I discovered they weren't my only audience that evening. Bryan had made his way onto his terrace – attracted by the sound of Over The Rainbow wafting up from the river as the sun began to go down.

My saxophone was an indispensible partner every moment of that journey. I was happy. Angela was happy. Our hosts were happy. Even the turkeys seemed to be happy!

\*\*\*

Back in Grand Junction, we took the train to San Francisco – where John Coltrane was waiting for us. Sunday at the Coltrane Church brought together everything I had gone through so far in the first six months of life with a saxophone – and a whole lifetime as a fan of the music.

It was an intensely spiritual moment as well as being one of the greatest highlights of my life. And I don't believe there's any way it could have been achieved without the unconventional road I'd been following. My lessons with Björn and even those difficult early weeks with Raymond had all played their part. But so too had my time in the Sicilian sunshine and even more so the opportunity to play in such beautiful natural surroundings as I was experiencing right here in America.

I started to recognise that the road I had been following was so much broader than just learning an instrument. It was more a way of life. And the most important thing of all was that I wasn't learning to play like someone else. After only a short time, I was discovering my own way of playing the soprano – my own sound. And in this I found an echo of the wisdom of Coltrane's final vision:

"Expression."

***

As we travelled we were colliding with expression in so many forms.

So far as music was concerned, San Francisco provided an opportunity to spend time in the Haight Ashbury district soaking up the vibe of the Sixties psychedelic rock that had been another of my top musical inspirations. It was music free of the restrictions that had gone before, music that drew on a variety of traditions, music that reflected the freedom of Coltrane.

A freeform solo by Grateful Dead guitarist Jerry Garcia contains much of the same spirit as Sixties jazz; Carlos Santana followed the mammoth success of Abraxis with Love Devotion Surrender – an album of Coltrane tributes; The Allman Brothers' Duane Allman famously claimed he'd learned everything he ever needed to know from Miles Davis's Kind Of Blue – the 1959 jazz classic featuring Coltrane on sax.

We had also been soaking up visual arts all along the way from New Mexico to California – especially the work of Native Americans inspired by their shamanic traditions. Alongside that we were reading the works of the beat poets and a whole rainbow of expression from a host of American bards.

And most importantly, apart from expression in the arts, we were surrounded by the expression of the natural world. We moved on from San Francisco to the Yosemite National Park – surely one of the greatest concentrations of natural wonder on Earth. We would explore this awe-inspiring landscape and at every moment be reminded of the divine expression of nature.

Nature is expression. Music is expression. Life is expression.

***

It was a beautiful but difficult drive as we headed out of the park to explore one last corner of the Sierra Nevada wilderness before our final night together. Tomorrow I would drive Angela to the ashram and we wouldn't see one another for six weeks. We thought about staying on Lake Tahoe but we drove around and it didn't appeal. In the end we opted for Truckee – which we had liked the look of when we passed through on the train. It was a good choice.

"So are you ready?" I asked.

"Absolutely. This has been such an amazing trip. But it can't go on forever."

"Think you'll cope OK?"

"I'll get used to it. I need to take the next step. You too."

"Not sure exactly what I'll do over the next week or so. But I'm looking forward to some quiet time before I head off to Atlanta."

"It'll be a bit like the ashram – except you'll have your music."

"Sounds good."

Little did I know just how prophetic our conversation would turn out to be. Even as we prepared for time apart, our inner journeys were already converging.

***

In the morning we drove to the ashram. It was a gorgeous location and even more remote than I had thought, right at the end of a series of unmade tracks. Angela was very satisfied with her lodging in a small hut down by a lakeshore and we were both happy to discover she would have a free day just a week later, even able to leave the site if she wished. We decided I would drive back and fetch her so we could spend a little time together before I left the area.

Then I headed back to the edge of the Sierra Nevada and tiny Nevada City, where I had decided to stay for the next 10 days, renting a room in a house in the nearby woods. I didn't know what to expect. But as I tentatively negotiated my way down dead end tracks and roads to nowhere, I realised this was a magical corner of paradise. And when I finally pulled up outside Susan's gorgeous house, it was clear I'd made the right choice.

Susan was away – and would be for most of my stay, leaving me with the run of her luxury designer pad. But downstairs tenant Jane was on hand to show me around. I knew I must be in the right place when her husband showed up wearing his Grateful Dead T-shirt!

The heart of the house was a huge space with sprung wooden floors and beams, 10 metres by nine metres and five metres high, featuring sliding glass doors along two sides that led onto a massive terrace skirting all around the house beneath the canopy of the forest. I stared up at the ceiling. There was only one thing on my mind – the incredible sound it was going to produce.

And sure enough the acoustics were as amazing as they looked. Once again I had fallen on my feet. Here I was, buried in the heart of a natural paradise in a gorgeous wooden sound box, more like a recording studio than a home stay. Within five minutes my sax was out of its carrying case and I was blowing for all I was worth. This was going to be one hell of a week.

***

The following morning I decided to explore, pulling on my trainers and heading out for an early morning run. I found plenty of forest trails and soon chanced upon a small stream to follow the course of the valley. There was nobody else to be seen as I explored folds of tranquillity all around me.

Just as playing the saxophone had been a kind of gift to myself at the age of 60, so I had started running when I was 50. Before then I could scarcely have claimed even the most basic of fitness. But I jumped into my new passion with enthusiasm and was soon taking it quite seriously – timing my runs, planning daily training sessions, taking part in races. Does any of this sound familiar?

Just as with my sax playing, I had set regular targets – it was a personal challenge. But eventually I realised there was something even more important than timings or positions. It was the joy of running itself that was counted. It seemed like I had already reached a similar point with music.

That morning my running was at its best – the way I had come to appreciate it. I wasn't running fast, I wasn't running in a race, I wasn't running far, I wasn't even running with a particular destination in mind. I was just running.

And as I ran, I noticed all the little details of the forest – the trees, the leaves, the bushes, the grass, the stream, the earth, the sunlight, the colours, the smells, the temperature, the air, the breeze. I was no longer thinking about running, I was no longer thinking about where I was running. I was simply moving through space, using all my senses to engage with the moment.

That is the best kind of running or walking or swimming or sitting because it's about acting with intention – being mindful. It's a liberating experience and I felt blessed that morning to be liberated from my thoughts enough to fall into such a space. But even as I ran, I allowed a silent soundtrack to play inside my head. I knew that running and playing were pretty much the same thing.

Back at the house, I felt tired. But I knew I had to play. I got through two marathon sessions and it seemed that my playing was more fluid than ever before. The sound was good. Between sessions I took a break to draw for a while, again just letting the process flow.

When I had finished I went out onto the terrace and for the first time I decided to play Amazing Grace. It felt good.

*\*\*\**

The time had come to explore the backcountry in the more remote corners of the Sierra Nevada. I threw some bottles of water and a picnic into the car together with the sax and a sketchpad and drove into the hills. The drive was longer than I had expected through a beautiful but empty forested wilderness, passing a scattering of tiny settlements. I was aiming for Packer Lake where I had located a trail that would take me up to the Sierra Buttes Lookout.

By the time I arrived it was already midday and I realised I would struggle to get back before dark if I stuck with my original laid-back plan. So I gulped down my sandwich, left the drawing kit in the car and strapped the sax to my back. I knew my priorities – even when about to go trekking in the mountains.

I was completely alone. As I stepped away from the car my isolation was complete – and that suited me fine. Just to be on the safe side I put a note on the dashboard with the time and my planned route. But what I had in mind involved just me, the mountain and my music.

I made good progress for an hour or so to reach a shady lake where I sat down for a break. I was just admiring the view and about to take out my sax when I heard voices approaching. It turned out to be a couple out for a hike – I wasn't quite as alone as I had thought.

"Howdy. So what's that you've got on your back? You out hunting?"

"Hi there. Actually, it's a saxophone."

"You don't say. You find that's useful out here?"

"Who knows?"

"I guess. Well, have a good day."

"And you."

I allowed them to get ahead of me on the trail so I could regain my solitude. Of course, I also took out the soprano and played for a while, allowing its sound to ripple across the lake and float back among the reeds and trees. Just as I had imagined, the stillness brought yet another dimension to what I heard. I wasn't sure if it was the sound I was making or my appreciation of the sound that was starting to change. Perhaps it was a bit of both.

As I continued my musical journey, progressing through new environments both indoors and out, I began to recall the work of Paul Horn. I was still a teenager when I first heard an extract from his incredible album Inside – on John Peel's late night radio show – playing solo flute in the dome of the Taj Mahal, notes tumbling, resonating and bouncing around that legendary space.

It begins with Hindu chants echoing through the interior as Horn whispers the take number into his microphone. Then he takes out his flute and starts to play, the sound scattering in waves to the far side, eventually washing back for him to play along with the echo. The haunting voice returns, a spiritual invocation spiralling above. At times flute and voice intertwine, at others Horn's flute flies unaccompanied in multiple circuits around the dome.

Just like Coltrane's solo in My Favourite Things, many of Horn's most captivating sequences bring to mind the flight of a small bird as it circles overhead, flitting from tree to tree. Sometimes I think the process of learning to play is the closest I'm likely to get to having my own wings.

Already an established jazz artist at the time Inside was recorded in 1968, Horn had recently trained in transcendental meditation alongside The Beatles at Maharishi Mahesh Yogi's ashram in India and was inspired to strike out in a new direction of atmospheric soundscapes. It was a watershed moment for him as he went on to record in a host of wonderfully resonant locations around the world both on flute and soprano sax. As my own sound experiments continued, the spirit of Paul Horn (who had only passed away a year earlier) stood shoulder to shoulder with the grand master John Coltrane.

After playing for a short while, I packed the soprano away and began the toughest part of the hike – straight up a rough track towards the jagged peaks high above.

There are towers dotted all around the mountains in those parts, which in the not too distant past were used as fire lookouts. Their function has since been overtaken by satellite technology but it was one such lookout I was now aiming for. As I continued to climb it seemed an impossible distance away.

Eventually I joined the broader track of the Pacific Crest Trail and soon realised this would have been an easier climb from a more accessible parking area. But I would have no option but go back the way I had come in order to pick up my car. My focus was increasingly on how long it would take to get back and then drive to Nevada City. I was running short of time.

As I continued upwards I calculated that I probably still had just enough daylight to make it to the summit and then return home in safety. But it was clear that in order to do so I would have to forego the main purpose of my day – playing from the top of a mountain. It didn't take long to decide what was more important so I set about finding an alternative to the summit.

Among the trees I glimpsed an area of rocks well away from the trail and made my way towards it. I clambered up and soon discovered that I was in fact heading for an alternative summit – a high point that was still some way below the fire look out. It was in a perfect position, well away from other potential hikers but with a commanding view across the vast mountain range. It seemed like I could see for hundreds of miles. I took out my sax and started to play.

The joy of that moment is hard to put into words, transcending all language or even thought. I had no concern what anybody might think. I didn't even worry what I might think. I played recognisable melodies and attempted to improvise as much as my limited abilities would allow. But in the end it wasn't even the sound I was making that was important. It was my connection with the wilderness, with the chunk of nature that filled my view as far as I could see.

I was playing on top of the world, breathing in pure mountain air and breathing out a stream of notes. It was as simple as that. I don't know how long I played. But it was long enough. And when I had finished I just sat for a while longer in silence, utterly content. Then I packed away my instrument and started the long walk back. Mission accomplished.

It seemed natural to be on my own in all this but I didn't deliberately avoid company and after a while I chanced upon the same couple I had met earlier. They were now with another hiker heading along the PCT to get a lift back to their car. They too were worried about the time it might take to get back.

"So did you make it to the top? What an incredible view that was!"

"Actually I decided to stop before I got that far."

"Well you sure missed something there."

"I guess so."

"Hey, was that you playing your saxophone?"

He turned to address the other hiker. "This is the guy we were telling you about."

"I'm sorry if I disturbed you or anything."

"Are you crazy. It made our day. Have you any idea how beautiful it was to hear that music floating around the mountaintop. You a professional?"

I shook my head in disbelief. "No way."

"Sure sounded like it to us. Didn't it guys?"

So that's how the Sierra Buttes ended up as yet another unscheduled public performance – and a hit at that. Once we had said our farewells and I was trudging back to the lake, I began to wonder if it would ever be possible to play like that in front of a real audience. Now that really would be a challenge.

Both the Coltrane Church and playing on the mountain had been magical moments along the road – moments beyond almost beyond consciousness. But would they end up meaning anything in the overall scheme of learning my instrument? And did it really matter? Perhaps in its way what I had experienced was more important than music. I had a lot to think about on the long drive back to Nevada City.

***

The town itself was one of the most pleasant small rural American settlements you can imagine. The more I explored, the more I realised just how difficult it would be to tear myself away from its relaxed charms. This wasn't a car town like so much of America. People still walked through the centre to visit shops, bars, restaurants, art studios, craft outlets and a scattering of new age businesses. Wandering the next day – a Thursday – I came across one such place offering free restorative yoga sessions – every Thursday.

It seemed too good an opportunity to miss. Angela had previously introduced me to the wonders of restorative yoga so I knew just what to expect as the instructor (also called Bob as it turned out) manipulated me into position for an hour of pure relaxation. I knew Angela would be engaged in her practice at the same time so it seemed somehow appropriate as we approached the end of our first week apart that we should come together in a shared a moment of meditation – even at such a distance.

Supported by blocks and cushions my mind slipped away from Nevada City, joining Angela in her ashram to survey the journey so far. I followed the flight of first one small bird and then two as they danced through my mind. We were at the halfway point of our year and it was all heading in the right direction.

Suitably restored, I found a small coffee house where a folk singer was making a fine sound. I took time out to listen before heading back to my house in the woods, where I continued to play, exploring fresh inspiration from the natural world. After a while I sat out on the terrace with Sanders, the Golden Retriever who was the only other resident at the time.

It was good to have another being to chat to as I finally started to draw my first picture while in the USA. Drawing had emerged as a new activity while I was in Sicily – the first time in my life I'd ever tried. But I didn't even have a sketchpad or proper materials at the time – I just started to draw in an exercise book. Impressions. Colours. Feelings.

This time I had come prepared with a proper pad and crayons. But I'd spent too long looking for something to draw and no time actually doing it. Now that I was sitting peacefully with Sanders drinking a glass of orange juice, I reached out for the pad and just started to draw what that turned out to be a glass of orange juice. Just as I had ended up doing in Sicily, I was drawing with ease, enjoying the process and watching the results emerge – the Zen of colour.

And my playing was heading the same way. In fact sometimes it felt like I was playing colours rather than sounds. It was a peaceful place – in its own way every bit as much a Zen retreat as any ashram. But I was never quite alone. It wasn't just Sanders who shared the house – as became clear when I caught up with Jane and husband Mike from downstairs later that afternoon.

"We just wanted to say how much we've enjoyed having you stay – and being able to listen to your music every day."

"I'm sorry if it ever got a bit to much for you."

"Not at all. It was a privilege. Loved every moment."

Either they were incredibly gracious people – which I am quite sure they were – or things were indeed going well.

It seemed to me that the secret I had stumbled upon was in playing with no motive or expectation. I was just playing. The sound was coming from within and was being made for no greater purpose than that. It was just Expression.

***

A week had already flown by and the time had come to fetch Angela for some precious moments together. I took her on my favourite forest walk, showed her around town and shared a massive brunch at my favourite restaurant. The interior of Ike's was filled with New Orleans memorabilia – posters, photographs, beads and masks – as if urging me on to the next stage of my journey.

Of course we also went back to the house to share my wonderful retreat in the woods. We had already shared a lot that week – including yesterday's meditation – even though we had been apart at the time. All too soon, we had to drive back to the ashram and I asked Angela if she thought it might be appropriate to take my sax along for the ride.

"Why not? In fact, I know exactly where you should play."

As soon as we arrived, we took a walk around the beautiful grounds. Angela led me around the back of the lake and up a small hill to a group of large rocks overlooking the rest of the site. It was a temple to Shiva, with sacred images painted on the rocks, a heap of small offerings and the remains of burnt candles and incense scattered all around. She looked at me and smiled.

"Will this do?"

I stared back into her sparking eyes.

"You bet."

It was the crowning glory of the first half of the American leg of our journey. I took my soprano from its case as Angela sat in a lotus position and let her eyes close. I took a few deep and even breaths in preparation and then started to play. I had no idea what would come out but the notes began to drift into the air and slide across one another, tumbling through the rocks. The notes themselves began to breathe and take on a life of their own, slipping into a version of Amazing Grace and then sliding apart into a mantra of peace.

It felt good to be playing once again at the top of a hill. It was starting to feel like this was the way of my journey – hiking with a saxophone and playing from the hilltops. It was an attractive idea – a kind of audio version of Tibetan prayer flags, scattering notes on the wind and allowing them to be carried into the valleys beyond. Maybe those notes would sometimes be heard by humans; maybe they would be heard by animals; maybe they wouldn't be heard at all. But that didn't matter. They were still there – carried by the breeze up into the sky.

I played for a while. Angela meditated for a while. As we walked back down the hillside, the people we met were all smiling.

***

Sicily had been about finding a new home, discovering its history, its culture and its food – soaking up what it was to be a Sicilian. Along the way I made a start on playing my saxophone without a guide – getting used to coaxing it to share its sound with me.

Coming to America was allowing me to get closer to the music. It seemed that by reaching out into nature I was starting to explore the instrument's inner spirit. At Angela's ashram I had reached the end of that chapter on a high.

But that wasn't all this leg of the journey would bring. What now lay in store was a return to the source. This was the continent where jazz was born. I was on a pilgrimage. And the music was about to take centre stage.

# CHAPTER TEN

## Birth of the Cool
## – A Road Trip Back to the Roots

A couple of days later I flew into Atlanta to pick up a tour group that I would accompany for two weeks through the Deep South. Once I reached the end of that tour I would pick up a second group to repeat the circuit. I was all set for a month on the road in the land that gave birth to popular music in all its forms – from the Country and Western of Nashville, to the Blues of Memphis to Jazz in New Orleans.

All tour leaders have their own take on things. But for me there was only ever one focus for this tour – music. I had even prepared a series of CDs to illustrate my commentary as we burned through the miles of tarmac that lie ahead. I was on the road again.

On the way out of Atlanta we shared tales of civil war in The Night They Drove Old Dixie Down; heading on through Georgia I just had to include Rainy Night In Georgia and Georgia On My Mind. Our first stop was Chattanooga – cue the Glen Miller Orchestra and Chattanooga Choo Choo.

Passing close by the legendary Muscle Shoals studios in Alabama, I put on a selection of classics recorded there – When A Man Loves A Woman, Mustang Sally, I Never Loved A Man, Brown Sugar – the selection could have gone on forever. Then we found ourselves on legendary Highway 41 linking New Orleans with Nashville and Chicago. So I slipped on the Allman Brothers Band's road trip special Ramblin' Man:

> My father was a gambler down in Georgia
> He wound up on the wrong end of a gun
> And I was born on the back seat of a Greyhound bus
> Rollin' Down Highway forty-one
>
> I'm on my way to New Orleans this morning
> Leaving out of Nashville, Tennessee...

And there we were in Nashville, country music capital, ready for a concert at the Grand Ole Opry, music bars on Broadway, the Country Music Hall of Fame and a visit to RCA Victor's Studio B – custom built for Elvis. That was the cue for the first stage of our Elvis Fest – alongside the likes of Roy Orbison, The Everly Brothers, Jim Reeves, Dolly Parton and so many others who had recorded there.

Next stop was Memphis – home of the blues, Beale Street bars, Elvis's mansion at Graceland and the original Sun Records studio where it all began both for him and for Jerry Lee Lewis, Carl Perkins, Johnny Cash – not to mention the likes of blues great Howlin' Wolf. Elvis's recording of That's Alright at Sun is generally quoted as the moment Rock & Roll was born – essentially a synthesis of blues and gospel from the black community with white country music. Further down the line in the 60s, Stax also built their studios in town to record the soul greats such as Otis Redding I had grown up with as a boy listening to Radio Caroline.

Another classic road cuts across the bars of Beale Street on its way through the blues country of the Mississippi Delta snaking its way down to New Orleans – flagged by Bob Dylan in his classic Highway 61 Revisited. But that wouldn't to be our route down to the Crescent City. We left the bus behind and hopped on board the train that lent its name to yet another song – The City of New Orleans.

The best thing about New Orleans on this tour – both for myself and the guests – was that plenty of free time had been scheduled, allowing ample opportunity to take in the ambiance of a city always at play. There's no shortage of music clubs and bars in the French Quarter and Frenchman Street. But they're just part of the story, with marching bands and buskers as you turn every corner. You don't have to go out and find music in New Orleans – it comes to you.

Even the funerals have a musical kick as bands weave their way through the streets in honour of the departed. It was a tradition that had arrived in Brighton the year before when Ian Price passed away, with local musicians taking to the streets to stage a traditional New Orleans funeral in his honour. Now I was learning to play on his old sax and I was determined to somehow pay my own small tribute to him while I was here.

***

The American Civil War gave birth to military brass bands and by the 1880s brass instruments had become commonplace in New Orleans; at the same time the blues were seeping in from the Delta both along Highway 61 and from the steamboats heading downriver; and finally syncopated rhythms of the old Sunday slave gatherings on Congo Square developed into Ragtime piano style. These were the three essential ingredients that combined into jazz in the hands of pioneers such as cornet player Buddy Bolden at the turn of the twentieth century.

Cornet and trumpet led the line at first – notables to follow including Bunk Johnson, King Oliver and Louis Armstrong. But other later instrumental voices included Sydney Bechet, who began on clarinet before switching to soprano sax. Naturally I visited the New Orleans jazz museum to gaze at his old soprano – which amazingly enough he had found while visiting London!

By the time jazz was born, the city had already fallen on hard times. Its huge wealth before the Civil War was a thing of the past and central districts were falling into decay, with the music developing around the bordellos of Storyville. The truth is that New Orleans was no more than the crucible for what went on to become jazz – by the early 1920s the music was already largely based in Chicago. Sydney Bechet left town in 1916, King Oliver in 1918, Louis Armstrong in 1922 – all part of the migration sweeping hundreds of thousands of African Americans away from southern segregation and towards economic opportunities in the north.

## THE JOY OF SAX

The music spread through major cities during the Jazz Age of the Twenties – Chicago, New York, Kansas City. By the 1930s New York's Harlem was the hub, with the likes of Duke Ellington and Cab Calloway forming big bands and launching Swing as the soundtrack for the nation's dancehalls.

The 1940s brought modern jazz in the shape of bebop – faster, more intense, more complex, no longer principally designed for dancing – from the likes of alto sax player Charlie Parker. The baton was passed on when he gave 19-year-old trumpeter Miles Davis his first big break. Miles went on to typify the modal cool jazz of the 1950s and during that decade the process of renewal continued when he hired John Coltrane to play in his band.

It was at this point in time that traditionalists began to look back to the origins of the music – they got left even further behind when the likes of Coltrane blew the lid off the remaining rules in the Sixties. For the first time since the birth of jazz, there was a movement that saw New Orleans as the ancestral home – arriving in pilgrimage to open traditional jazz venues in the French Quarter such as the Preservation Hall. The music had come full circle.

***

Preservation Hall is no more than a bare room where old-timers play the old tunes untouched by passing years. When I first visited the city back in the 1980s, you used to squat on the floor and put a dollar in the hat for the privilege. These days you need to stand in line and pay a hefty charge for a ticket to get in. Times change.

It was one of the original revival venues along with the likes of Fritzels in Bourbon Street. These and plenty more venues were still on tap when I arrived with my group, offering a taste of the old days for the price of a beer and something in the hat for the band. The Spotted Cat over in Frenchman Street was one of the best, with more than a nod in the direction of the original Preservation Hall.

But I also looked in at some more upmarket venues like Irving Mayfield's Jazz Playhouse at the Sonesta Hotel and the Snug Harbour – a tiny venue on Frenchman where Delfeayo Marsalis managed to squeeze in his whole big band. Delfeayo is a top trombone player and part of the New Orleans Marsalis clan that also claims brothers Wynton on trumpet, sax player Brandford, drummer Jason and pianist father Ellis. It was a night to remember. As was a visit to the rather eccentric Palm Court Jazz Cafe, set up by jazz-loving refugees from Kent playing alongside the cream of the old-timers.

## THE JOY OF SAX

After the Traditional Jazz revival of the Fifties and Sixties there came another equally crucial revival – and this time it arrived from within the city itself rather than courtesy of nostalgic outsiders. This was the brass band revival of the late Eighties and Nineties – still a vibrant subculture today. Whereas Trad largely remained in the hands of older performers and listeners, brass bands returned to vogue as an energetic youth-based street entertainment.

Back in the 1980s, I chanced upon one of the very first public performances by the Rebirth Brass Band as they snaked around a desolate Armstrong Park. Having inspired an entire generation of funky street performers, they were now back in a vastly improved Park 30 years later for a Community Festival.

And for me that was New Orleans at its best. While the purist traditional bands often left me cold, the younger and larger street bands retained the essence of the original while absorbing what had followed and also letting their hair down in much the same way their forebears had done a century earlier.

This was a music that oozed with the ingredient X that had attracted me to Coltrane and that I had even discovered in my own attempts at playing without boundaries. It was a music that incorporated form, freedom and fun – and I reckon the three Fs are what jazz is all about. It was a glorious noise.

In fact, you could easily go to New Orleans and never go inside a bar or concert venue and still catch some of the best music the city has to offer – out there on the streets. That's where the essence of jazz continues to flow and that's where I tracked down most of the best sounds. It also provided an opportunity. It seemed to me that with so much music going on out there, nobody would notice if just one more novice sax player showed up.

I was in search of a place to pay tribute to Ian Price and – if I'm to be honest – also to lay claim to having played in New Orleans. I didn't want to start competing with the buskers trying to make a living. But I did want to play in the heart of the French Quarter. And in the end I found exactly what seemed to be the perfect spot at the very centre of everything – in the park of Jackson Square right there in front of the cathedral.

I settled down on a bench and started playing a simple blues. It didn't have a name but it soon found its own groove before working its way into the New Orleans vibe. I couldn't help recalling Joni Mitchell's beautiful song For Free, telling how she had played to thousands in a packed concert hall while outside the people just walked by, ignoring an old man who was playing his clarinet on the street corner – and he played real good for free.

Whether I played real good is debatable but at least it was for free. My blues started morphing into some recognisable tunes, some of them returning more often than once. It all poured out as I continued to play for the next hour – Sonnymoon For Two, Blue Monk, Over The Rainbow, Stormy Weather, Stella By Starlight, My Favourite Things... Even O Sole Mio managed to creep in along the way. I was just about to wind up when one of the gardeners took time out from sweeping the leaves to amble across.

"Excuse me Sir. But you ain't allowed to play music inside the park gates."

So that was why I was the only one playing in such a perfect location! I obediently put my sax away – I was all done anyhow. But heading back out of the park I noticed the sign – No Soliciting. So I figured that playing music was actually OK – just so long as you played For Free.

\*\*\*

It was time to hit the road again. I was up early the next morning to check onward arrangements and oversee loading of the luggage. While waiting in the lobby for the porters, the lift doors opened and out stepped a man well into his Eighties wearing dark glasses and a red satin bomber jacket. I recognised him immediately – Jimmy Carter of the Blind Boys of Alabama. A member of his backing band wearing a similar jacket helped him across to the desk.

They had been playing a concert in town the previous evening and I couldn't believe my luck to have the opportunity to exchange a few words with such a legend. The Blind Boys were formed in 1939 from the choir of the Alabama Institute for the Negro Blind and have performed ever since – one of the greatest gospel bands of all time. And Jimmy Carter had been with them for most of that time. I'd first seen them perform at a party at the House of Blues when I was in New Orleans in the Nineties on a business trip and I'd seen them at every available opportunity ever since.

It's a good job Jimmy couldn't see me blush as I admitted to being one of his biggest fans. I thanked him for all the pleasure he'd given me over the years. He graciously thanked me in turn before a taxi arrived to take him on his way. It was a suitably musical farewell to such a musical town.

***

# THE JOY OF SAX

We drove west across Louisiana to the sounds of local Cajun music before crossing into Texas near Port Arthur – giving me a chance to play some Janis Joplin, who was born in the town. The following day we flirted with the joys of Western Swing – an infectious mix of jazz and bluegrass designed for the Saturday night dancehalls in rural Texas – before heading on towards the Mexican border and the Tex Mex of San Antonio.

Beer and the Blues gave way to Tequila and Mariachi. It's an infectiously upbeat kind of town with a party vibe – in many ways the Hispanic twin of New Orleans. Wandering away from the tourist hotspots of the Riverwalk, I came across a High School Mariachi contest in the cathedral square. I took in the music for a while only to be knocked out when an aging celebrity popped up for the second time in less than a week – the great Flaco Jiminez. As he stepped onto the stage I instantly recalled his accordion playing that was the highlight of Ry Cooder's classic album Chicken Skin Music.

The journey continued through Texas as far as Fort Worth. The only connection with jazz I could think of was that it had been the home of free jazz sax pioneer Ornette Coleman. But I soon discovered there was also now an excellent jazz cellar off Sundance Square with regular Sunday night jams. It was the perfect place to spend the final night of the tour.

***

Guests had occasionally heard me playing in my hotel room – and a couple of them even spotted me busking in Jackson Square. At the end of the second tour as we prepared to head for the airport to catch our flight to London, the requests began. They wanted to hear me play.

I finally gave into the pressure and marked my first eight months as a sax player with an impromptu lobby performance of Summertime, Somewhere Over The Rainbow and Amazing Grace. Was this yet another candidate to chalk up as a first gig? It was getting close – and all seemed to go down pretty well.

# CHAPTER ELEVEN

## Intermezzo II
## – A Brief Return

With little more than a month for a pit stop back in Brighton – including the Christmas holidays – there wasn't a lot of time for further musical adventures. And to cap it all, I arrived with a classic dose of long-haul sore throat. Nonetheless, only a couple of days after touchdown I found my way back to the arches behind the station to meet up with Björn. It felt good.

Sadly, it was immediately apparent that my sense of rhthm hadn't improved much while I had been away – although I did just about manage to play along with his piano accompaniment. On the upside, I had taken a big step forward in terms of sound and expression. It was clear where I was coming from.

Just to settle into the groove, we ran through a couple of the old tunes – Over The Rainbow and My Favourite Things. I played over Björn's piano and seemed to pass the test. It was time to move on to something new.

By a wonderful coincidence, he had chosen a tune by Sidney Bechet – Si Tu Vois Ma Mère. Having tracked down Bechet's ancient soprano in New Orleans and started to develop an interest in his music, it was a perfect selection. As an added bonus, Björn introduced the piece as part of the soundtrack to Woody Allen's Midnight In Paris. It was a film I didn't know. But I soon put that right and discovered both a musical and a cinematic gem.

The lesson actually represented a major step forward – the first time we had based an improvisation on the individual chords of a tune. This is a fundamental part of the art of jazz improvisation. Sadly, as ever, I learned there was a big gap between theory and practice. And yet it was an inspiring session. At the end of a long spell on the road, it allowed me to sense more of the way ahead.

The following day, my sore throat started to kick in some more and I was forced to ease off. Even when I started to recover I realised there was still a massive ocean to cross in terms of my playing. During the lesson I had glimpsed a glorious musical world out there. But left to my own devices on a rainy day, my confidence came crashing down again.

It was a month later when Sonny Rollins came to the rescue. This was to be my final lesson with Björn for a few months. We were about to set off for South-East Asia so he gave me a free choice. I opted for Rollins' calypso classic St Thomas. It was tricky at first but once it clicked I found a connection that has never been lost.

Sonny Rollins is another musical hero. Right up there with Coltrane. I had seen him play a live solo set in London a few years earlier when he was already in his Eighties. He was dynamite!

The memory ensured I was a particularly enthusiastic pupil that cold winter day under Brighton railway arches and I've carried his little jewel of St Thomas around the world with me ever since.

# CHAPTER TWELVE

## Into The Jungle
## – Asian Trails

The Asian leg of the Year of Sax began in style. For the first time, Angela joined one of my tour groups. She chose well. This was the easily the most luxurious of all the tours I had ever led – a cruise up the mighty Mekong from Vietnam into Cambodia.

There's something a little unsettling, a little contradictory, about cruising into the heart of darkness in a luxury riverboat. That ultimate war movie Apocalypse Now was based on Joseph Conrad's novel Heart of Darkness with good reason – that is exactly where the journey upriver takes you. Cambodia is one of my favourite places on the planet largely because it is itself such a huge contradiction – a place to love and hate with equal passion. There are no half measures.

And it's infectious. The vast majority of tourists I have ever taken to this part of the world used to tell me they had come to see Vietnam but left with Cambodia in their souls. There's simply too much joy and too much pain to leave anyone untouched. A history that ranges from the cultural highs of the Angkor temples to the horror of the Khmer Rouge Killing Fields merges into a politically dubious present.

The country has an unequalled spiritual legacy, with ancient Hindu and Buddhist temples bursting through the canopy of what precious little remains of the jungle after intensive logging by the ruling kleptocracy. Visitors cannot fail to be charmed by the ubiquitous peaceful chants of saffron robed monks; the people are among the friendliest and most placid you will meet anywhere on the planet. But those at the top and bottom of the pile have very different stories to tell. This is a country of extreme wealth and extreme poverty – a country where luxury cars cruise past naked and deformed beggars on every dusty street. But despite everything, it's a place that's impossible not to love.

This was the third part of our year away. The first had taken us to Sicily in search of a new home – a transformation from the old life to the new, bringing with it a sense of rebirth. The second in the USA was a journey through time to discover more about the music. The third would hopefully take us deeper into the spirit. This was my time to flow in harmony with Angela's own journey.

For Coltrane the spirit had been every bit as important as the music. It was the crucial fourth dimension. We were now heading into the unknown – in many ways we really were entering the Heart of Darkness.

***

Phnom Penh was a city I knew well and soon after arriving we made for the best of all vantage points – the terrace of the Foreign Correspondents Club. From there it was possible to survey all the bustling activity that throngs the banks of the Tonle Sap early in the evening.

We had walked past the river's branch with the mighty Mekong and paused opposite the Royal Palace where offerings are made at the end of each day. A line of flags fluttered in the breeze as sunset softened from red and gold to the gentlest of purples. A tall mast towered above the shrine where devotees laid the lotus flowers they had bought at the market just along the riverbank. As ever, a group of young monks lounged by the river, willing to explain the mysteries of their nation.

"It was right here that many years ago a flag in the shape of a crocodile was found in the river. And during our Buddhist Holidays it always used to appear on a flag pole," we were told.

"Then the spirit of the flag, Preah Ang Dong Kar, took the form of a four-armed Buddha and was given a home right here in the shrine next to the mast. We give him offerings to make sure the magic of the river will never dessert us."

And the magic is very special as the Tonle Sap is the only river in the world that reverses it's flow each year, emptying into the Mekong in the dry season before filling and flooding the land up country when the waters of the Himalayas pour down to replenish it. That is the secret of the fertility of the Cambodian basin and its ancient civilisation, with all the wealth created by abundant agricultural production allowing excess labour for temple building. According to Khan, the guide I had employed for our tour group, it was an over-enthusiastic reading of ancient history that had inspired the Maoist revolutionaries of the Khmer Rouge in the 1970s.

"They thought they could recreate the Ancient Empire. All they needed to do was destroy the modern world and put everyone to work rebuilding the irrigation systems that had once created such huge riches. But they were cruel. They gave guns to peasant boys and put them in charge. They killed our people. They killed my parents. They killed my uncle and then my brother.

"This we should never forget – we can never forget. But those in power now, they also have blood on their hands. The people know this but we don't want the killing to return. So we keep quiet."

Gazing out at the end of the day from the FCC is a bit like that. Silence and noise. Pleasure and pain. You watch the chaotic traffic and the people scurrying by, glancing along the riverbank towards the shrine where Buddhist monks have gathered to pray. Nearby, people buy small birds so they can whisper a message to be carried up to Heaven. The moment fills you with the peaceful spirit of a remarkable nation. And then you recall the Killing Fields.

It's a bit like Sicily and the Mafia or the USA and Slavery. All three countries have a stain that's impossible to shift. They are about so much more than that. But they all carry a label that sticks, despite having so much joy to offer.

"How do love and hate get so mixed up?" asked Angela.

I took a sip of my Angkor beer.

"Maybe that's what we need to try and work out while we're here."

***

This was clearly the leg of our journey for dealing with big issues. So we decided we should wash away the good life we had been enjoying on board the cruise ship before settling down for our stay. With that in mind we signed up for a week of intensive yoga and meditation in a jungle ashram. It didn't turn out quite the way we had in mind.

As soon as we arrived, we were introduced to a young devotee who listed the house rules and insisted on immediate advance payment for a week's stay plus various additional charges. We were then shown to a Spartan hut that seemed in imminent danger of collapse. We had missed the main meal at lunchtime so were left to our own devices until evening prayer and meditation.

The guru was away so a devotee called John led the prayers, suggesting we should all be grateful for the experience. The only thing either of us gained that first evening was a rash of mosquito bites.

After a fitful night of sleep among the local insects and rodents, the bell rang well before dawn to prepare for morning yoga. Angela was in her element. I was struggling as ever but did my best to distinguish between a down-facing dog, an up-facing cat and a ruptured penguin.

Yoga was followed by a lengthy meditation, at the end of which we had an opportunity to survey the other inmates – all westerners, all young and all utterly docile. Perhaps it was down to the fact we were well above the target age range but we were clearly the only ones prepared to actually question any of the institutional regimentation with which we had been presented.

"You'll get it after a day or two. It's all designed to help your spiritual journey. The guru is utterly amazing," beamed one clueless youngster. We never did "get it" though.

By then we were utterly starving, looking forward to lunch with an unnatural zeal. So we grabbed our plates and stood in line to tuck into the delicious vegetarian meal we had been promised. But as the queue advanced, we looked at the shrinking bowls on the table and rapidly understood the catering hadn't been planned with the same level of care as our strict timetable. All the best bits were scattered on the top of each serving bowl so those at the back were in for meagre pickings.

Sure enough, by the time we got to the table all the tomatoes and other toppings were gone from the salad, leaving a shrinking bowl of plain lettuce. I wondered if it was just my lack of the discipline and self-sacrifice needed for ashram living. So I shrugged, figuring I'd probably over-indulged on the cruise ship anyway. But Angela had more experience in these things and wasn't feeling quite so compliant. She marched up to John and pushed a plate of limp leaves under his nose.

"Look at this. There aren't even any tomatoes left."

His smile exuded spirituality and self-belief.

"That's Karma," he said.

The prospect of spending an entire week surviving on nothing but lettuce wasn't the most enticing of prospects. And unlike Angela's California ashram, I wasn't even allowed to play music – although bizarrely enough there was a corner of the garden where smoking was allowed. Such were the crazy rules. I wasn't at all sure I could survive. In the end we decided to take it a day at a time and do things in our own way, determined not to leave before the amazing guru put in an appearance to share a little enlightenment with us.

Lunch the next day wasn't much better – although this time we did join the race for the front of the queue along with all the others who didn't quite trust to Karma. The day after, we managed to borrow a couple of bikes with dire warnings that we were responsible for their safety. It didn't matter. We were happy as we cycled through beautiful countryside to a nearby village market.

We left the bikes by the side of the road and explored. This turned out to be the most wonderful experience of all our time at the ashram. We did our best to communicate with the women squatting on the ground and eventually managed to track down some delicious snacks such as fried plantain and sweet dough balls. We had found a kind of Heaven after all!

We wandered back to the bikes smiling for the first time in a couple of days. Except the bikes weren't there. Disaster! And we had been specifically warned to take good care of them. There would be trouble back at the ashram.

We looked all around in terror until a local man who spoke a little English came across to ask if he could help.

"Our bikes. They've been stolen!"

He smiled.

"I don't think so," he said. "Things are not stolen here. That is not our way."

"Then where are they?"

He pointed across to a fenced-off area filled with carts and bikes. And sure enough that's where we found them. Wasn't Cambodia wonderful? Our confidence in human nature fully restored, we cycled back to the ashram to be greeted by John in a state of great excitement.

"Guess what? The guru. He's back. He will take the evening meditation. You'll finally get to hear him speak."

That evening we settled down among the mosquitoes to await his grand entrance. Long after everyone else was assembled an aging American hippy strode into the yoga hall from his luxurious private quarters at the bottom of the garden to sit on the large throne reserved only for him. We both listened carefully but by the end of the week we were still no more enlightened than when we had arrived.

***

The next day we hired a tuk-tuk for the short drive to Siem Reap and the room we had rented online for the rest of our stay. Any advance booking made blind is always going to be a leap of faith. You'd better hope you got it right if you plan to spend a couple of months in someone's home without knowing anything about them.

Actually I had managed to tease out a couple of important facts in advance. First, the house was well outside the busy centre of town in a relatively secluded area. That was positive. Secondly, just like us, one of our hosts was Italian and the other English. It sounded promising.

What we weren't prepared for was our Karma finally lining up in a hugely positive swing. Valentina and Steve were not just great hosts – they went on to become lifelong friends. But most remarkable of all, it turned out that Steve was a professional sax player. What could be better than that?

And it all kicked off as soon as we walked in through the gates on that very first evening.

We found ourselves in the midst of preparations for a barbecue, with bottles of ice-cold beer thrust into our hands before we could even drop our bags. The evening unfolded with great food, great conversation, great company and – best of all – great music. Once the meal was over a succession of brilliant musicians got up to play.

## THE JOY OF SAX

There was Tony, a hot alto player who had just arrived from Singapore. He had even played with Sinatra and Dean Martin in his time and was now blowing up a storm even after consuming several bottles of white wine. There was Christian, trumpeter and musical director who now lived and played permanently in Siem Reap with his Cambodian wife. And then of course there was Steve, who on the night played a cool duet with French guitarist Andre and was also about to play a crucial part in my infant musical education.

It looked like what we had trailed as being the purely spiritual part three of the Year of Sax was already morphing into possibly the most musical experience of all – one where the musical and spiritual had a chance to breath the same tropical air. Perhaps some kind of enlightenment was on the cards after all.

# CHAPTER THIRTEEN

## Cambodia
## – The Zen of Sax

Siem Reap had mushroomed from the dusty little town with a couple of guest houses I had first visited 15 years earlier into a major tourist destination with mile upon mile of five-star hotels – all on the back of the remarkable jungle temples of the Angkor civilisation built between the 8$^{th}$ and 13$^{th}$ centuries.

Visitors are drawn by the lure of Angkor Wat – one of the world's great archaeological wonders, situated just beyond the gates of the ancient city of Angkor Thom. At its peak this was the greatest city in the world with over a million inhabitants and at the heart of one of the greatest empires ever known.

The majority of visitors today remain unaware of the sheer scale of temple building that took place in the area, covering many hundreds of square kilometres. As with any famous location in the days of mass tourism, the places listed in the guidebooks crawl with tourists while dozens of even more remarkable spots remain hidden in glorious obscurity.

The allure for visitors is largely based on opportunities for sunrise selfies against a backdrop of ancient stone temples hidden in the jungle. The most popular location of all is probably Ta Promh, where the trees and creepers have reclaimed the space to grow right through the temple walls. It's a setting straight out of the movie Tomb Raider – although these days it's pretty tough playing at being Angelina Jolie alongside the tourist hoards.

It was the ancient cult of Devaraja – the God King – that led to such a proliferation of temples throughout the region. Each king needed to build a temple in his own lifetime so that when he died, he could join with the deities to protect his people from above. Originally dedicated to Hindu Gods – especially Shiva or Vishnu – there was later a switch to Buddhism, followed by a Hindu revival before finally settling on a permanent Buddhist practice.

But that was all long ago. The bottom line is that Siem Reap has developed into a fun town to service the tourist boom. The nearby sites all get incredibly crowded. But if you time it right or are prepared to wander further afield, the experience can still be profoundly spiritual. The temples remained an inspiration for us both. And Siem Reap was a fun town to spend some time. But I have to say that the single most important place during our two months or so in town was the oasis of Valentina and Steve's Garden.

***

Our room had a large balcony overlooking the length of it and the following morning I stood there for my first short session playing a few old favourites – Sonnymoon for Two, Over the Rainbow, Summertime, My Favourite Things.

The skyline shimmered in the haze – we were approaching the hottest time of year – and exuded a strong sense of the exotic. It was a sensation underlined by the traditional timber build of the balcony and the sound of chanting filtering across the landscape from nearby Buddhist monasteries. I started to improvise on a state of mind, playing my instrument as a meditation. It felt good – even though I still had far to go if I was ever to approach mastering it.

We soon settled into a daily routine. I used to get up at dawn when the air was still relatively cool and ran through the dusty streets in a loop down to the river and back. Angela would encourage me to join her in some gentle yoga and meditation once I got back – although as time went on she would head out to share and teach her practice with others. I was largely left to my own devices in the garden, writing a little, drawing a little and playing saxophone a lot.

At first I was fairly timid about the process – not wanting to disturb the neighbours with my tentative noodling. But as time went on it became clear that nobody was too bothered and my sounds began to merge with the everyday sounds of Cambodia. The only thing that stopped me was when I heard Steve practicing, realising he packed more into a single scale than I could dream of managing in all the tunes I knew.

But in general I was feeling pretty pleased with progress – pleased enough to devote several hours a day to playing. Maybe it was just the incredible surroundings or the fact that the soprano works pretty well as a solo instrument. But I was getting a sense that it sounded pretty good. I still had a clear belief I would struggle to play when I got together with real musicians. But I was happy enough with the sound I was making. And that made it all worthwhile.

It was a few days into our stay that Steve suggested having some lessons with him. Wow! By then I'd realised his cv was no less impressive than Tony's. He'd backed the likes of Sammy Davis Jr and Barry White, enjoyed a successful stint playing dance clubs in Spain and worked on cruise ships around the world before finally settling down in Cambodia. And now he was offering to give me lessons in his garden!

The best thing Steve did was to take me straight back to basics. He set up a backing track on his computer while we played together through a major scale. After a while he had me haltingly working through them all in turn.

"This is the key to everything," he said.

"You need to play those scales again and again and again. You need to get them inside your fingers so that they're printed into your muscle memory. That way you'll be able to start picking up little tricks in every key."

I knew he was right. It's the stage I had missed when I played guitar as a teenager – and paid the price. It was too much like hard work and I had similarly been avoiding going there this time around. But now I was determined to move on.

Cambodia would be my time to nail the scales and build a foundation for what was to follow.

I worked and worked on those scales every day. Every so often I'd allow myself time for a tune and a chance to use parts of the scales as a little flourish or a mini solo. I'd been making a reasonable sound for a while but now I was finally choosing notes that worked with each other. I was starting to put things together.

Another session with Steve reminded me of the wonders of blues scales –another complete set of 12 to commit to muscle memory. It was a subject I had touched on long before with Björn but I'd managed to forget all about it by then. I knew that if I really worked on them this time around there'd be no forgetting them again. They were among the most powerful resources I would ever learn.

The same lesson also introduced me to the circle of fourths (or fifths – depending on which way you look at it). This simple but beautiful annotation of all the keys was another fundamental resource that would forever stay by my side. I was gaining a few reliable companions.

It was at this moment that I began to appreciate the stunning beauty of the relationships between all the notes and keys. The circle was far more than a wonderful learning tool. It was a mandala of sound – a tool for meditation that meant even more in a garden surrounded by the chanting of nearby monks.

The next day we went even deeper into blues scales, breaking them down into riffs that could be used in a solo. The material I was picking up each day was getting more and more powerful. And best of all was the way Steve was boosting my confidence, telling me he couldn't believe I'd been playing for less than a year. He said I was way ahead of the curve, claiming not to have properly learned his own scales until he was well into his career, relying for many years on sight-reading to play in big bands. I'm not sure I ever quite believed his modesty.

Every so often guests would appear in the room next to us. With wonderful timing, a Chinese couple with impeccable English arrived on the Eve of Chinese New Year. Tommy and Wendy headed straight to the central market and prepared a New Year's feast to remember. It seemed like another signal that things were heading in the right direction – an auspicious moment for new beginnings.

I decided this was surely the time to push my musical education even further along the line. So before I had time to change my mind I fired off an application and payment to join a four-day residential jazz workshop back in the UK over Easter. I think I was probably trying to make up for lost time as I was now in more of a hurry than ever.

When Chinese New Year dawned the next day, Angela and I went for a long walk, counting our blessings for everything that had already come to pass during the year and looking forward to whatever else might be in store. But when I finally got around to practicing that afternoon, I realised my confidence had its limits as a steady stream of musicians arrived in Steve's flat downstairs. I didn't dare play once I heard them run their impeccable scales.

The last to show up was Tony, looking much the worse for wear. But as soon as he put his horn to his lips he played like an angel. Just like a true jazz musician, I thought to myself. My confidence ebbed back as he took a break and I started to play up on the balcony. We took turns, eventually trading riffs, Tony down in Steve's flat and me up above. In a traditional timber-frame Cambodian house that's as good as sharing the same stage.

It was only later that I discovered Tony had been there because he was taking over Steve's gigs as he wouldn't be able to perform for a while. He'd gone through some local dental treatment, which had gone disastrously wrong and left him unable to play. He would have to go back to Europe for a few weeks to get it fixed.

Before leaving, he generously took me through even more material to work on while he was away, moving from a scale into an improvisation on the same scale. Tony also became a regular visitor, working through Steve's songbook, both on his own and with a guest vocalist. It was a privilege to be allowed to sit there soaking it all up as they prepared for the coming series of gigs.

Steve and Valentina left for Rome and we were left in charge of the house, garden and cats – quite an honour after only knowing them a couple of weeks or so. The garden felt more than ever like my own private domain while Angela more often than not was out with a growing network of yoga buddies. Every few days we would walk into town so I could join the sunset class she was teaching at a local hostel – perfect after a long day of blowing scales.

In the meantime, I realised I had jumped in way out of my depth when it came to registering for the jazz course. I received a list of 12 tunes – three of them for each day. I was expected learn to play them by ear and then be ready to improvise over them.

Blimey, I thought. That's impossible.

I made further enquiries and was told the course was perfectly suitable for beginners. I decided to stick with it. But in truth, the peace I had found in my playing was melting away as an undercurrent of panic began to set in.

I started working through the minor scales and had a go at one of the tunes for the course – My Funny Valentine. It just happened to be Valentine's Day and it didn't sound so bad. As ever, I was a sucker for any positive signs.

No pain, no gain was the new mantra. I didn't stop to wonder what had happened to the old one of music is fun. Hopefully it hadn't gone away forever.

***

Siem Reap felt increasingly like home as we settled in and got to know the local ex-pat haunts. We were out most evenings to catch what live music we could – Tony's jazz gigs, lounge music in the hotels, Christian's residency in a local beer garden, grunge rock at the X Bar. There was even a homecoming concert by international Cambodian rock band Dengue Fever. Good times.

In the meantime I began studying some musical theory and realised just how little I knew. The course back in the UK would be so important in finally getting to grips with it all. I knew there was plenty of hard work to be done if I was going to be ready. But it would be worthwhile.

When Steve got back, his teeth were still not up to playing but he generously led me through a gentle 12-bar blues that we felt might fit one of the 12 tunes I was now desperately studying. We also knew our time in Cambodia wouldn't last for ever and there was still so much that we wanted to do beyond the immediate world of that perfect Garden. In particular, I wanted to explore some of the more remote jungle temples.

We devoted a whole week to unearthing some real beauties, travelling from one site to another with yoga mats and soprano saxophone in hand. The great thing about the less visited temples was that we could always find a quiet corner all to ourselves. We would unroll the mats for some yoga or meditation in an idyllic setting. Then I would take out my soprano and play.

Best of all, I could forget about theory, scales and the looming course. I could just focus on that sound again as I had done back in the wilderness mountains of California, connecting with the environment. The most important musical lesson I had learned from a year of travelling was also one that was such a clear feature of Coltrane – sound is everything.

In a way this was a return to the adolescent guitar playing I had regretted for so long. But I was eventually coming round to the idea that technique and theory can be overrated. What comes first – the sound or the music? I was desperate to continue my musical journey but that didn't mean I couldn't feel good about what I had managed to achieve so far.

I knew I would continue to work on all the other aspects of music making – including the hard bits. But I felt I had perhaps managed something even more important. I had connected with my instrument. I had found a sound and it was my sound. It seemed to me that this was something I could cherish and take with me as I continued along the road.

***

But before we could leave, another road was calling. Again it would lead me through the jungle and past many of the temples, allowing me to experience them at their most atmospheric one last time. I had enjoyed my early morning running routine throughout our stay. So when I noticed posters going up for the Angkor Wat Marathon, it seemed they were reaching out to me.

I may have been used to running early in the morning. But in order to avoid the worst of the heat, the event was scheduled to start well before dawn. When the day came, that meant setting my alarm for 2.30am for a tuk-tuk ride out to the temple complex. As I rode through the dusty streets I wondered if I was the only one in town crazy enough to run in the middle of the night.

But then we started to slow down and found ourselves surrounded by traffic – with jams all the way to the temples. Once we made it through to the starting area and the noise of revving tuk-tuks began to fade, it was an unforgettable experience with hundreds of competitors milling around one of the most atmospheric locations on Earth. And in the misty pre-dawn light there was an extraordinary sense of being transported back to the beginning of mythical time.

As I mingled with the runners – a mixture of Cambodian locals and visitors from all around the world – there was a sense that we were engaging in something special. This was no ordinary race. As we jockeyed for position at the start line, a sense of calm drifted across the moat from the temple and I felt we were tumbling back through the centuries to the games marking its dedication to Shiva. What an honour to be among those chosen to run.

We set off at a gentle pace around the moat and on through the trees to the gates of the ancient city of Angkor Thom. It didn't seem like a race so much as a meditation, a gentle sweep through the trees and those magical remnants of one of the greatest civilisations on Earth.

I wouldn't describe myself as particularly sporty and certainly never followed an athletic lifestyle for the first 50 years of my life. The benefit of all those years in a bar drinking beer rather than playing team sports only became apparent when I finally took up running. At a time when my contemporaries were queuing for knee surgery, I found that my own bits and pieces hadn't yet worn out – leaving me with a few more years to enjoy.

So the discovery of a fully functioning body relatively late in life came as something of a surprise. After a brief obsession with running faster and further, it didn't take long to realise that just having fun running was the only way that made sense – one pace at a time, one breath at a time, staying within the moment, exploring and enjoying the environment as it drifts on by.

Anyone who has tried to get into meditation and given up will know the frustrations of sitting uncomfortably with legs crossed, desperately trying to clear their mind to think of –

nothing. It's tough. And no wonder most people find themselves composing a shopping list to the accompaniment of snores from neighbouring devotees who have managed to drop off in the process.

It seems to me that consciously trying to clear your mind to think of nothing is the wrong approach if you want to achieve the undoubted benefits that meditation can bring. The key is being in the moment and not allowing yourself to shift through time – either backwards or forwards. To do that effectively, it works to think of something rather than nothing – even if it's just a small thing. Even better for me is to do a small thing.

Of all the practices you might learn at an ashram, I always preferred walking meditation. It works for me. And I guess running fits into the same category – only better. What I had discovered in recent years was that any activity can simultaneously bring huge gains physically, mentally and spiritually.

I can only imagine that taking up a physical activity at a younger age might have led to other priorities – such as winning the race. But I was starting to feel comfortable with my age and discovering that what I might have once found alien was now possible to embrace – but in a totally different way. I had discovered the pleasures of running mindfully. It was the same lesson I had been learning with music. All the streams were flowing together.

Just as I did in the California woods, I was feeling good as I jogged my way past creepers hugging the crumbling walls of a thousand-year-old temple complex, the sun beginning to crawl its way above the trees. It didn't even concern me to notice a steady steam of local runners taking shortcuts or grabbing lifts on passing mopeds.

It actually felt more than good. It felt divine – a truly beautiful experience. All I had to do was keep on running and enjoy every last twist and turn of this incredible course – to breath in the intoxicating smell of the jungle along with all its history, culture and spiritual traditions.

I was on a journey and it was a journey without end. I had no particular destination in mind. I was growing in my belief that the journey itself was enough – running, breathing, smiling.

It was the music of life.

# CHAPTER FOURTEEN

## New Guru New Message
## – The Brighton Connection

After a brief stopover in Hanoi we arrived back in Brighton to some bad news. Björn had moved home and was now living 40 miles away in Hastings – so there would be no more musical visits to the railway arches. But at least I had the Easter Jazz School on the horizon.

I packed all my remaining practice time with a desperate effort to prepare those 12 tunes as far as my meagre abilities would allow. I was struggling with the material just for Day One – Beautiful Love, Shady Side and Jumpin' With Symphony Sid. There wasn't much time left and seemed like I had a mountain to climb. It was perfectly clear I wasn't yet ready for such a huge challenge. But at least I was trying and perhaps I could learn something along the way.

Sure enough, the first day turned out to be an unmitigated disaster.

On arrival we were divided into four groups of 7 or 8 students ready for school principal Ronnie and the rest of his teaching team to start working with us. Even though I had clearly been put into the absolute beginner's stream, I immediately realised the school's concept of a beginner was very far from my own. I was completely and utterly lost as the dots on the sheet music started dancing in front of my eyes and I found myself unable to follow any of the tunes I had so patiently prepared.

I soon made friends with the students around me, who were extremely supportive. But that didn't stop the sense of sheer panic that continued throughout the day. I felt the tears welling into my eyes.

Help! Beam me up, Scotty! Get me out of here!

The day was split into four sessions – each with a different teacher and a different tune. The only time I stopped sweating was during Mark's class – the least demanding and most supportive of all the teachers. Most importantly for me, he didn't feel a need to drag us through the entire tune as written on the sheet music – Beautiful Love. He was more interested in helping us get a feel for the piece, encouraging us to find a few notes that might guide us through a simple improvisation.

That was more like it. But as soon as he was done, the next class was tougher than ever. How was I ever going to survive four whole days of this? I was ready to give up.

Two young women playing keyboards on the far side of the room were struggling almost as much as me. They helped me feel I wasn't completely alone. My heart sank the following day when neither of them turned up. I knew I should follow suit and walk out the door. But in the end I was persuaded to carry on – I would be on my own for the rest of the course as the class dunce.

This was pretty hard to take after all the hard work I'd been putting in over the past year. It seemed like I should be further ahead than this. But of course there's a big difference between playing scales on your own in a tropical garden and trying to play as part of an eight-piece band.

It didn't get any easier during the next couple of days, confirming that this was entirely another level from anything I'd attempted so far. Probably the biggest technical problem I faced was that I had never learned to sight-read music. That left me at a distinct disadvantage and I knew it was something I was now unlikely to ever completely overcome. But given enough time I hoped I might at least learn to cope a little better.

It seemed to me that my other big problem hadn't changed at all over the past year – I still had no sense of time or rhythm. I asked Ronnie for his advice.

"You're wrong," he said. "Who told you that anyway?"

"Well... There was Raymond. And then there was Björn. Even Miss Grant when I was a kid. In fact, anyone who ever tried to teach me music."

"Well, they're all wrong. You do have a sense of rhythm. In fact you have a particularly strong sense – there's a powerful pulse in your playing. Maybe it's too strong. The problem when it's so powerful is that it fights against the rhythm – the rhythm of the rest of the group. You just need to tame it."

This was clearly a polite way of saying that my timekeeping was even worse than I had ever imagined – I was in fact a completely hopeless case. But I let it go. I was way out of my depth – largely a result of consistently skipping over the basics in favour of having fun. Perhaps I should lower my horizons and just carry on enjoying life in my own sweet way.

I knew I was struggling so far as sight-reading and timing were concerned. But when it came to improvisation, making a glorious noise and a bit of expression then I was ahead of the curve. Whenever I got a chance to let rip with a solo – mainly in Mark's classes – I knew I could make an impression. But when I was trying to simply keep up with the tune I was floundering.

So in the midst of feeling like an abject failure, there was still a kernel of something precious for me to hang onto. I had a hunch that the things I seemed to do best were precisely those things that brought individuality to music. Maybe I was just kidding myself. But that is what I dragged from the wreckage of my musical career at the end of what had been an exhausting, challenging, intensely depressing but in its own way rewarding experience.

***

Actually, there turned out to be something even more important that I gained from the Jazz School. A long journey home was facing me at the end of it all. But as I was booking my taxi to the station, I discovered that Mark also lived in

Brighton. So we shared the journey home. It was to be a trip that changed my musical life.

Mark is quite simply an inspiration. Born with no left hand and fingers missing on the right, most people would have felt a career in music was simply a step too far. But Mark isn't most people.

Without fingers, there were very few instruments he could have considered taking up as a child. But with special adaptations and a series of attachments he was able to play the trombone and pursued his passion to the extent of becoming one of the finest jazz trombonists in the UK. Not content with just playing, he also went on to become an inspirational teacher with that essential ingredient – fun.

We talked a lot about music and I admitted that I was only just reaching the end of my first year of playing. I told him how hard I had found the course and how depressing it was that I didn't seem to be getting anywhere. He kindly expressed surprise that I was so new to playing and revealed he was running a series of group courses for mature students in Brighton.

"It's an introduction to Jazz improvisation – a whole cycle of modules which should take about a year to get through. If you're interested I'll let you know when I start a new group."

It sounded like the perfect way to continue my musical education – if only it weren't for the fact that we would soon be heading back to Sicily and I would also be away for big chunks of the year taking tour groups around the world. I started to realise the long-term practical prospects for learning an instrument on the road weren't terribly straightforward.

More than ever we were unlikely to spend many extended periods back in Brighton. Perhaps as my Year of Sax drew to an end my short musical career would also begin to fade. But Mark and I enjoyed our chat and exchanged numbers. It seemed unlikely that anything would happen soon but I was already looking forward to meeting again and taking the next tentative step.

***

By the time we did meet I had already been back to Sicily, led a few tours in the USA and Asia, celebrated another birthday, worked on my musical timekeeping with some new computer software and treated myself to a wonderful Italian hand-crafted Rampone and Cazzani saxophone. My excuse was that if I was going to have two homes then I needed two instruments. It also happens to be a wonderful instrument and a joy to play.

In order to make up for lost time, I made my way to Mark's house close to the railway station – only a few hundred yards from Björn's arches – for a couple of private lessons to cover the ground I had missed in his first block of Jazz Nuts and Bolts. It was brilliant.

I felt incredibly lucky to have found such a wonderful teacher. But most remarkable of all, it turned out that there was a link between my two most important teachers. Mark and Steve had been friends from way back – regularly playing together over 30 years earlier as members of the National Youth Jazz Orchestra of Great Britain. With Steve in Cambodia and Mark in Brighton I had unwittingly become the only connection between them. Fate, Karma, call it what you will. There were some powerful forces at work.

And as it turned out, my time with both of them was only just beginning. Mark certainly had a lot more to offer. So far as the Brighton connection was concerned, there was plenty more to come.

"Next time you're back, you'll hopefully be able to join the four weeks of Nuts and Bolts part two – playing in a minor key.

But next week I'm running a one-day workshop with lots of my regular students. You ought to come."

He looked me in the eye. "The great thing with a big group is that there's plenty of covering fire!"

It turned out to be a revelation, with over a dozen students playing a range of instruments and Mark coaxing an incredible performance from the ensemble. It was a joy for everyone – with none of the panic that had plagued me during the Jazz School.

And he was quite right. When there are enough people playing it doesn't really matter if you fluff a few notes. There's "covering fire" to get away with it and self-confidence takes care of the rest. In fact, that was an important part of Mark's method, which came with a complete lack of criticism or too much tough stuff, lots of encouragement, fun – and plenty of biscuits.

Another crucial development was that I found myself entering a local network of like-minded students. Although most of the others were well ahead of me, they were still on a journey of discovery. I found I was soon sharing a wonderful sense of comradeship with them. This is one of the great things about learning to play an instrument or returning to one later in life – there are so many other people doing exactly the same thing.

And once you find yourself on the edge of a network, it can only continue to grow.

One of the rocks of the workshop had been Ali, whose double bass playing had kept us all firmly on track. She approached me during the tea break –which was naturally accompanied by unlimited biscuits – with a proposal.

"I'm starting a regular jazz jam next week at a scout hut. I thought you might like to join in?"

I looked behind me in case she was talking to someone else.

"You mean me?"

I couldn't believe anyone could seriously consider me capable of such a thing.

"Of course. That was a great solo just now."

Easily flattered, the following week I found myself at the inaugural meeting of the Ringmer Jazz Jammers and had a blast. I didn't let on to Ali but the covering fire was an especially attractive feature of the afternoon.

***

Following another short spell away I joined a group in Mark's house for my first experience of Jazz Nuts and Bolts. It was a revelation as he led us gently by the hand for our first steps along the wonderful road of jazz theory. He had such an easy and encouraging manner that nobody even realised what a complex world we were entering. His skill was to make it all seem so simple and coax us along with the magic.

Once again it was over tea and copious biscuits that he made his move.

"I think you should also come to Saxshop."

"What's that?"

"It's been running for years and I'm helping out at the moment. It's a workshop but only for saxophone players – lots of them – loads of covering fire!"

His eyes twinkled.

"Sounds interesting," I said nervously.

"You'll need to sight read of course – which is something you do have to work on. And then there'll be an end of term concert. I'm sure you'll have fun."

## THE JOY OF SAX

Once again I would be jumping in at the deep end – joining half way through the term, relying on my non-existent sight-reading, playing alongside a bunch of far more experienced musicians and after just a few weeks standing up in public to play a concert. I hesitated and Mark moved in for the kill.

"Of course, there'll also be biscuits..."

***

The following Tuesday evening I took the bus to a community centre in a remote corner of town. It didn't look promising. But once inside, I discovered around 25 saxophonists had assembled into a large circle around teachers Beccy and Mark. This is going to take some organising, I thought to myself.

I immediately sought out the other soprano players. I was going to need cover from my own battalion if I was going to survive the evening in one piece. This was my first experience of playing music arranged into parts. In other words, we wouldn't all play the same notes at the same time. Each sub-group had its own music to follow, hopefully meshing into a glorious orchestral whole.

This was going to be tough. But at least the sopranos were a single unit. I quickly realised that my best bet was to hide in the middle of them so I could clearly hear what they were doing and try to play along. It didn't always work but it was a good strategy, with the stronger players helping me along.

The hard part for teachers and students alike was getting the arrangement to flow. But luckily Mark also programmed some work on solos in smaller groups. Apart from when the chocolate digestives came around, that was the only time I managed to relax all evening.

Against the odds, I managed to attend four Tuesdays out of the 10 scheduled for the full term. Before I knew it the end of term concert had arrived. It was to be a Sunday afternoon at the Brunswick – one of the best jazz venues in town. And it wasn't just any Sunday. It was December 11. If he hadn't already passed away, it would have been my father's birthday.

***

We all arrived early to squeeze onto the stage for a final rehearsal and a quick run through with a professional rhythm section of piano, guitar, bass and drums that had been brought in for the occasion. Altogether it was a very big band. After a break for the audience to come in and settle it was time for the houselights to go down and the concert to begin.

We launched straight into a Ska version of Christmas favourite Walking In The Air before moving onto the big brassy sounds of Hey, Big Spender. Then it was one of Mark's compositions People Watching People. Mid-way through he nodded energetically in my direction. My big moment had arrived and I let loose with my first ever solo together with a 30-piece backing band. Wow!

I switched to automatic pilot, trying hard not to think of all the things that could go wrong. I knew only too well that it was too late to do anything except go with the flow and accept whatever might come out. It was over before I knew it. But finally I knew what it was all about and couldn't help beaming with pride. That felt good!

Once the number was over, Mark generously picked out the soloists for applause. "Give it up for Bob on soprano – playing his very first gig!"

I was on Cloud Nine as we cruised through Moanin' and Enjoy Yourself to complete our brief set. The more experienced players had prepared additional material to continue in smaller groups. I was happy just to sit back and listen with that big satisfied smile still plastered across my face. I had achieved everything I had set out to do and so much more.

The Year of Sax, which had begun with my own 60$^{th}$, had led as planned to a first gig within two years – and it even turned out to be on my dad's birthday. But in the meantime a parallel universe had opened up in Sicily where a second musical life was also beginning to blossom.

## CHAPTER FIFTEEN

### The Music Goes On
### – Rocking All Over The World

The first part of our Year of Sax had already born fruit. We had gone in search of a new home and found one. It hadn't taken long to realise that Sicily was the place of our dreams. But we also recognised that Cefalù was not for us. A tour of the island led us to Siracusa and on our return we set about unearthing a permanent residence in its historic island quarter of Ortigia. It took time and a few false starts. But in the end we found the perfect place.

Of course, there was work to be done – we had to strip everything out for a total renovation. Luckily we had met Peppe by then. Not only was he a brilliant guitarist with a love of Bossa Nova, he was also a top builder. We recruited him and he set to work with a local team to construct a new home for us.

And then my phone rang.

"Hi. It's Valentina and Steve. We're in Sicily. In fact we'll be in Siracusa this afternoon. Can we meet up?"

What was going on? This was a completely separate part of the Year of Sax. But here we were with two worlds colliding. Perhaps there was a divine arranger out there and we were due some harmony from our travels.

It turned out that Steve's dental problems weren't over yet and he had been in Rome for more treatment. In the meantime, Cambodia's attractions were fading and they too were looking for a new home. We had been giving Sicily a good press so they decided to come and take a look for themselves. To cut a long story short, they liked whet they saw and decided to make the move.

By this time, we had discovered the Tana di Gufo – a tiny local pub where Peppe would pick up a guitar to accompany his wife Giuliana's joyous singing. It was far too small and intimate for a saxophone but Steve brought along a flute, which worked well. And a steady stream of musicians used to drift by – including another brilliant guitarist called Ettore.

## THE JOY OF SAX

One day at the building site, Peppe told us that Ettore had hired a disused disco where there would be some live music tonight. We should come along. That evening we met up with Steve and Valentina and made our way to Ettore's cellar bar.

We had allowed for Sicilian time by not arriving until 9pm. But it was still practically deserted at such an early hour. It was a wonderful cave-like space. A drum kit had been set up on the stage, where Ettore was already strumming a guitar through a powerful amplifier. We ordered a beer.

Moments later Peppe poked his head around the door.

"Hi Peppe, When does the band arrive?" I asked naively.

He looked at us and shook his head in disbelief.

"Where are your instruments?"

"Err... Well... We hadn't actually thought about..." I stammered.

"That's OK," He smiled." There's still plenty of time. You can go home and get them."

I looked at Steve. He nodded. "So long as the beer's still here when we get back."

We hurried through the labyrinthine alleyways of Ortigia to fetch our saxophones. Maybe it was no big deal for a pro like Steve. But I was feeling distinctly nervous.

By the time we got back and had downed another bottle of beer, a few more musicians had turned up to jam. We stepped up onto the stage and I had no idea what to do next – further handicapped by a total lack of the Italian musical vocabulary used by the rest of the band.

"What key do you think this is in?" I whispered to Steve.

"Not sure. Maybe E minor."

It seemed to work. Like at the Coltrane Church, I managed to find a comfortable spot at the side of the stage where I could hear myself play but couldn't actually be heard by anyone else. But just like the Coltrane Church there was a microphone staring at me from the front. And after a while Ettore started smiling and nodding at me to step forwards.

What the heck. What's the worst thing that can happen Let's just have a blast.

So I stepped up and started to play, desperately trying to recall some of the tips I'd picked up from Steve, Mark and Björn. Suffice to say all the good stuff went straight out the window in the heat of the moment. But I still had my scales to fall back on – especially the blues scales – and I managed to get into the grove. My time in a Cambodian garden hadn't totally gone to waste.

Hey, this is fun. I'm playing in a band!

I only played a couple of numbers but Steve stayed on stage and was of course quite brilliant. What was wonderful for me to realise was that nobody seemed to worry if I wasn't all that good. The only thing that mattered was playing and having fun. And it turns out that there are plenty of opportunities for this wherever you might be in the world. Musicians are incredibly open and encouraging people. This was an important lesson to learn. As was the fact that the best music comes when you forget about being nervous and just play!

We didn't know it at the time but this was to be the first night of many. When we met up with Ettore a few weeks later, he announced he had taken a lease on the premises and would be opening a permanent venue for live jams. This was great news. I'd had such a great time on that first evening once I'd pushed back against the barrier of my inexperience. I was ready for more of the same.

The other thing we didn't realise was that the grand opening of NAKA was in fact a reopening. Ettore had previously run another club of the same name, which had been closed down when the neighbours tired of loud all night jam sessions. Peppe had good reason to remember the final night.

"It was pretty late and I wasn't even playing. But when I stepped outside, someone threw a bucket of water over me from the window above."

Before long the new NAKA was operating four nights a week. Ettore could turn his hand to playing pretty much any style of music – so one night might be reggae and ska, one night classic rock, one night heavy metal. But Wednesdays were reserved for jazz.

Having discovered that I knew Sonny Rollins' St Thomas, he used to insist on playing it with me at the start of the evening. Peppe's love of bossa nova meant that he soon suggested learning Blue Bossa. And on the first night Giuliana stepped up to sing Summertime. So I soon had a fresh repertoire and before long could turn my hand to some of the other simpler pieces.

I continued travelling, working and popping over to Brighton. But back in Sicily I managed a few lessons with Steve and we had some good nights of jamming at NAKA. But all too soon the inevitable happened.

It may not have been the jazz nights that were the problem. Personally I suspect it was more to do with heavy metal sessions through the night with volume set to 11. Anyhow, NAKA was closed down once again. The locks were changed and another musical adventure was over for Ettore – and for the rest of us in Ortigia. It had been good while it lasted.

While NAKA had been a short-lived experience, it had opened up the world of Sicilian jam sessions for me. And they didn't completely disappear. Every so often there would be a party and musicians would bring along their instruments. One summer evening Ettore's auntie even threw open her musical instrument shop for a jam. There were lots of good times to savour.

***

For a while, I had realised there was a growing conflict between my continuing world travels and a growing passion for music making. One reason for choosing the soprano in the first place was that it was more portable than other members of the saxophone family. But it wasn't portable enough – and it was too loud for practicing in hotel rooms. I needed another instrument.

It didn't take long to realise that the logical answer was the flute. A lot of sax players take up flute as a second instrument

– just like Steve. And I'd always had a weakness for gentle meditative music – like the works of Paul Horn that had floated back to me when exploring the Sierra Nevada in California. Coltrane's soprano and Horn's flute had something in common in terms of the spiritual heart of the music that I had unearthed over the past year or so.

I bought myself a flute and once again went through the challenges of playing a new instrument. Although the fingering is similar to the saxophone, it's different enough to catch you out. And because it's in concert pitch, I had to transpose everything I played. I told myself this was good for my musical development – and my aging brain cells.

I also invested in a mini electronic keyboard, brought my guitar out of retirement and picked up a cane Sicilian whistle when we came across a group of traditional folk musicians while we were on a tour through the interior. My musical repertoire was expanding. With a second saxophone in Brighton, I was able to continue my development on twin fronts.

And then the opportunity arose to bring the two worlds together. Mark had started to organise a few residential workshops and we started to kick around the idea of staging a workshops for a group of his Brighton students in Sicily.

Angela and I set to work organising accommodation, venue, instruments – even Ettore's auntie came on board to provide the double bass we needed.

We were even planning a concert by the students for the final evening and a jam session with some of the local musicians. I was looking forward to what would have been the culmination of my musical adventures in two worlds. Everything was in place.

But then the first few cases of Covid-19 arrived – and then a few more. Before we knew it, both Italy and the UK were in lockdown. The workshop had to be cancelled – or at least delayed.

It was a step backwards. But the music helped me get through those difficult times. Mark took his classes online. So it was possible to see more of him than ever – both from Brighton lockdown and from Sicily. Suddenly there were no borders to my musical education. It was available wherever I had a WiFi connection.

Mark even put together a series of virtual recording projects encouraging his students to jam to the same backing track and then assembling the results. Our musical world continued and once the lockdowns started to ease he instituted a new venture in Brighton with the Jamboree Jazz Orchestra. And the Sicilian workshop is set to finally come around in the very near future.

***

The one thing I knew from that period was that it was more important than ever to share the power of my musical odyssey. I realised that if I could do it then others could too. And the whole thing was continuing to be such a wonderful adventure, delivering its benefits and joys every single day.

It's hard to be precise about what it has done for me – for my personal relationships, my inner self, my world. There's no doubt I feel nourished by what I have gone through. But I am more convinced than ever that it is a mistake to seek specific results. Learning music is like any journey – like life itself. The journey is more important and more enriching than any particular destination can ever be. The river flows through it, allowing us to improvise in a variety of keys and styles along the way.

I chose the path of the soprano saxophone with John Coltrane as my guide – the joy of sax. But there are many other paths and many other guides. If we find the right road, we can follow it over the hills and far away. Who know? Maybe even somewhere over the rainbow...

# THE JOY OF SAX

BOB SWAIN

THE JOY OF SAX

All the events in this book took place as described and to best of my recollection – although I have altered a number of names to protect identities. However, three important characters are for real and remain in these pages under their own names – Björn, Steve and Mark – the musical guides who set me off along the road to Saxophone Heaven. My wonderful wife Angela is also very much for real and has remained my guide and companion throughout. These four deserve all my thanks and gratitude for being there to push me along whenever I needed it most.

## Also available by Bob Swain:

## Tracks Across Africa

In 1988, the author set off on a year-long drive from Brighton to Dar Es Salaam – following in the tracks of Humfrey Symons, who made a very similar journey some 50 years earlier. Tracks Across Africa is an account of both expeditions, detailing their incredible experiences along the way and the profound and lasting impressions left by their respective adventures.

## Timbuktu: Prince Of Stars

The novel of Bob Swain's animated feature film project Timbuktu – a magical African adventure for children and young at heart following a whirlwind of myth and sorcery through the heart of the Sahara Desert.

## Blood On The Mekong

A novel set in South-East Asia, combining ancient myth and 20$^{th}$ century history with an adventure of self-discovery. After the death of his wife, Jake Simpson goes travelling, desperate for escape. But while in Phnom Penh, he meets Oliver Robert and is captivated by a mysterious figure who has lived and seen too much. When Oliver dies of an overdose, his death becomes Jake's obsession. His journey follows the Mekong River, flowing through its historical tributaries – the Vietnam War, the bombing of Laos, CIA drug running and the Pol Pot years in Cambodia. The parallel story of American pilot Sam Campbell reveals an amoral but passionate exploitation of the heroin trade in order to fund America's secret war in Laos. When Jake's pursuit of Oliver's ghost finally leads him to Sam, he is confronted by the godlike self-belief of one who has controlled the destinies of millions.

Printed in Great Britain
by Amazon